Cool!

Berufsvorbereitung Englisch – BEJ / VAB

von
Birgit Herrmann
Andrew K. Johnson

Ernst Klett Verlag
Stuttgart · Leipzig

Cool! Baden-Württemberg – Englisch für BEJ und VAB

Das komplett überarbeitete Cool! führt gezielt zum nachgeholten bzw. verbesserten Hauptschulabschluss Berufseinstiegsjahr (BEJ) bzw. dem Vorqualifizierungsjahr Arbeit und Beruf (VAB). Exakt nach dem Lehrplan in Baden-Württemberg werden mit Cool! alle geforderten Kompetenzen (A2 im VAB bzw. A2+ im BEJ) und Prüfungsformate trainiert. Cool! ist ebenso ideal für junge Erwachsene in außerschulischen Kursen geeignet.

1. Neuerungen auf einen Blick

- **Komplette Neubearbeitung** der Schülerbuch-Inhalte, der Konzeption und des Layouts
- Von Anfang an werden die **Prüfungsformate intensiv trainiert**. Die *Test training*-Seiten bereiten auf die Abschlussprüfung vor.
- Im Mittelpunkt aller Units steht die **Kommunikation im (Berufs-)Alltag**; dabei liegt die Betonung auf dem Verständnis von gesprochenem und geschriebenem Englisch.
- Unterschiedliche Schülerkenntnisse erfordern starke **Differenzierung**:
  - nach unten durch multimediale und interaktive Online-Übungsaufgaben (*Üben interaktiv*)
  - nach oben durch Auswahlmöglichkeiten zwischen verschieden schweren 1 und 2 Aufgaben, *Extra exercises*, berufsrelevante *Jobsites* oder Vokabeltrainingseiten.
  - weitere Aufgaben und Hilfen zur Differenzierung im Lehrerhandbuch.
- Motivierendes **Multimedia-Training**:
  - Download des **Talking Vocabulary** als MP3-Daten über die Cool!-Codes zu Beginn jeder Unit.
  - 7 **BBC-Videos** zum Training des Seh-Hörverstehens. Dabei wird das authentische Material durch grafische Vokabelhinweise zum leichteren Verstehen entlastet.
- **Grammatik** wird in kleinen Einheiten wiederholt und geübt.
- **Vokabeltraining** pur:
  - Vor allem **jobrelevante Vokabeln** werden – neben der Wiederholung des Grundwortschatzes – sukzessive eingeführt und trainiert.
  - Da die Vokabeln bereits auf jeder Seite erklärt werden, sind die **Vokabeltrainingseiten** *(Vocabulary)* im Anhang konzentriert auf das jeweilige Thema mit begleitenden Vokabelübungen.
  - Über den Cool!-Code kann ein **Compact dictionary** Deutsch – Englisch kostenlos heruntergeladen werden.

2. So sind die Units aufgebaut

- Einstiegsdoppelseite **Entry/Audio**: Vorbereitung auf das jeweilige Lehrplanthema durch interessante Bildmotive bzw. humorvolle Hörverstehensaufgaben.
- Doppelseite **Text** übt das Leseverstehen – mit eingebettetem Skills-Training.
- 2 Seiten **Interaction** bereiten im Besonderen auf die mündlichen und schriftlichen Kompetenzen in der Praxis vor.
- Ausstiegsseiten **Exit** vertiefen ausgewählte Grammatik-Themen: Die Lernenden können dabei selbst überprüfen, ob sie die entsprechenden Regeln richtig (zu Ende) formulieren können (induktive Grammatik). Außerdem wird das Unit-Vokabular wiederholt. Hier ist auch als optionale Variante die **Video lounge** eingebettet.
- Die Doppelseite **Extra exercises** dient der weiteren Grammatikvertiefung und Differenzierung.

- Es werden alle zu erreichenden Kompetenzen und Prüfungsformate wie Leseverstehen, Mediation und Guided Composition auf der Doppelseite **Test training** intensiv trainiert.
- **Anhang – Cool! tools**
  - **Job-Seiten** vermitteln die wichtigste Lexik attraktiver Berufe.
  - **Vokabeltrainingseiten** bündeln thematisch die wichtigsten Vokabeln, begleitet von Übungen, zuzüglich Grundwortschatz und alphabetischem Vokabular.
  - **Klappumschläge** bieten wichtiges Sprachmaterial wie Phrases, Zeitenformen, etc. auf einen Blick.

3. Variante **Keep Cool!**

Keep Cool! ist die leichtere Alternative zur Vermittlung von Basis-Englisch (A1).

Lernhilfen

Ziel:	Lernzielformulierungen: Ich weiß, warum ich das lerne.
Vocabulary:	Vokabelfokus
Grammar:	Grammatikfokus
flat Wohnung	Vokabelerläuterungen in der Randspalte
2	anspruchsvolle Aufgabe
EXAM	Prüfungsaufgaben von Anfang an
Video lounge	Authentische BBC-Videos zum Training des Seh-Hörverstehens

Symbole

A1.12	Hörverstehensaufgabe oder Lesetext, Track 12 auf Audio-CD 1 im Lehrerhandbuch
V1	Original BBC-Video
f6en95	Cool!-Codes: kostenlos unter www.klett.de 1. Downloads: Talking vocabulary (vertonte Wortlisten) als MP3-Daten, Cool! compact dictionary (die komplette Wortliste Deutsch – Englisch) 2. Üben interaktiv: Multimediale Online-Aufgaben zu Differenzierung und Selbststudium
Example	Beispiele, Musterlösungen
→ G1	Verweise auf die Grammatik im Anhang

Inhalt

1 Turn me on

Ziel: Ich kann sagen, was ich regelmäßig mache. *Beispiel: I listen to music. (simple present)*

A What are Carlo's and Ella's hobbies?
Was sind Carlos und Ellas Hobbys?

1 What do you think? Who likes Nicki Minaj and Eminem?

____

2 And who likes Katy Perry and Justin Bieber?

____

Vocabulary: **Über Hobbys sprechen**

cook, dance, do sport, go shopping, hang out with friends, listen to music, read, surf the internet, watch TV

Grammar: **Was jemand regelmäßig tut** → G1

I read	**I often listen to music.**
you read	Ich höre oft Musik.
he/she/it reads	**Sue usually surfs the internet.**
we read	Sue surft meistens im Internet.
you read	**My friends watch TV all the time.**
they read	Meine Freunde sehen die ganze Zeit fern.

B What about you?
Und Sie?

I like ____________________

____

My favourite singer/group is ____________________

____

to turn on einschalten, anmachen
all the time die ganze Zeit
both beide
to hang out „abhängen"
favourite Lieblings-
singer Sänger/in

A bad day for BigDadDave

A **Listen to the story. Tick the right picture (1–3).**
A1.1 Hören Sie sich die Geschichte an. Machen Sie ein Häkchen an das passende Bild (1–3).

1  ☐

2  ☐

3  ☐

B **Listen to the story again. Tick *true* or *false* for sentences 1–4.**
Hören Sie sich die Geschichte noch einmal an. Machen Sie bei den Sätzen 1–4 ein Häkchen bei *richtig* oder *falsch*.

	true	false
1 Dave likes rap music.	☐	☐
2 Dave is usually good at his job.	☐	☐
3 Mary is Dave's daughter.	☐	☐
4 Ms Francis is friendly to Dave.	☐	☐

Grammar: to be → G7

I am	I'm
you are	you're
he/she/it is	he's/she's/it's
we are	we're
you are	you're
they are	they're

C **And what about Dave's friends? Circle the right form.**
Und was ist mit Daves Freunden? Umkringeln Sie die richtige Form.

Example:
→ *CoolCoCo* *are* *is* *a rap singer too.*

1 Paul like likes Eminem songs.
2 Joe and Emma are is metal fans.
3 Alicia often watch watches music videos.
4 Sabrina and her friend usually go out goes out dancing on Saturdays.
5 Asif has got a job. He work works a lot.

The test

A1.2 Ewa is a hairdresser. She has got a new job at *Hannah's Hair*. It's her first day today, but she already knows the rules.

Rules at *Hannah's Hair*:

Always be polite to our customers!

- Help them with their coats.
- Ask them if they would like a cup of tea or coffee.
- Never talk about other customers.
- Never use your mobile phone when customers are around.
- No MP3 players!

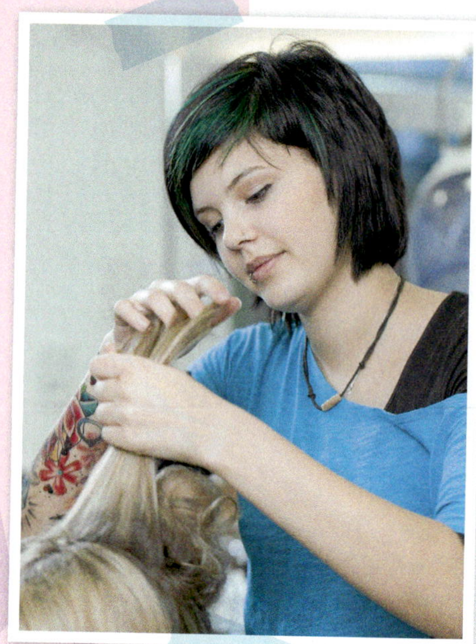

Ewa is sad. She loves music. And she loves her MP3 player. But she can't use it here. Here's Ewa's first customer.

Ms Hill	Good morning. I'm Ms Hill. I've got an appointment.
Ewa	Good morning, Ms Hill. Can I take your coat? … Thank you. Please sit down.
Ms Hill	Thank you. Now, I have to look good tonight. Can you curl my hair a little, please?
Ewa	Certainly, Ms Hill. Would you like a cup of tea or coffee?
Ms Hill	No, thank you. Tell me about yourself. You're new here, aren't you?
Ewa	Yes, I am. My name is Ewa. I live in Park Street and I love music.
Ms Hill	Park Street? Now, you must know that terrible Mrs Jackson. She lives in Park Street too.
Ewa	Yes, I know Mrs Jackson. She's really … er … Your hair is almost ready to dry.
Ms Hill	Good. You can listen to your MP3 player then.
Ewa	Oh no, I can't.
Ms Hill	Why not? I can see the earphones in your pocket.
Ewa	MP3 players aren't allowed here.

At this moment, Ewa's mobile rings.

Ms Hill	You young people and your mobiles. Go on, answer your phone. I'm sure it's important.
Ewa	I can't. It isn't allowed.
Ms Hill	You're a good hairdresser, Ewa. And you know the rules. Now go on, answer the phone. It's my daughter.
Ewa	Your daughter?
Ms Hill	Yes, my daughter Hannah – Hannah Hill, your new boss. Well done, Ewa! You've passed our test.

Vocabulary: Handys und Co.

- earphones, headphones, MP3 player, mobile (phone), smartphone, ringtone
- to answer the phone, to call/ring somebody, to send/receive a text, to text

hairdresser Friseur/in
already schon, bereits
rule Regel, Vorschrift
customer Kunde/Kundin
coat Mantel, Jacke
they would like sie hätten gern
around in der Nähe
appointment Termin, Verabredung
to curl kräuseln, aufdrehen
certainly sicher, selbstverständlich
almost beinahe, fast
to dry trocknen
earphones Ohrhörer
allowed erlaubt
Go on. Nur zu. Mach(en Sie) schon.
to answer the phone ans Telefon gehen
Well done! Gut gemacht!
to pass bestehen
headphones Kopfhörer
ringtone Klingelton
to receive erhalten
text SMS
to text eine SMS-Nachricht verschicken, „simsen"

Skills Tip

Lesen Sie immer zuerst gründlich die Arbeitsanweisung. Was **genau** müssen Sie tun?

A Finish the sentences. Tick A, B or C for sentences 1–4.
Vervollständigen Sie die Sätze. Machen Sie bei den Sätzen 1–4 ein Häkchen bei A, B oder C.

Skills Tip

Lesen Sie jeden Satz in der Aufgabe in Ruhe durch. Suchen Sie im Text nach Wörtern, die auch in der Frage auftauchen. Das kann Ihnen bei der Antwort helfen.

1 The rules say that Ewa has to

A ☐ help customers.
B ☐ talk about customers.
C ☐ use her mobile phone.

2 Ewa's first customer is

A ☐ Hannah.
B ☐ Ms Hill.
C ☐ Mrs Jackson.

3 Ewa's customer wants

A ☐ tea.
B ☐ coffee.
C ☐ nothing.

4 Ewa's customer is really

A ☐ Hannah's daughter.
B ☐ Hannah's mother.
C ☐ Hannah's customer.

B Match the English sentences 1–6 to the German sentences A–F. Draw lines.
Ordnen Sie die englischen Sätze 1–6 den deutschen Sätzen A–F zu. Ziehen Sie Linien.

1 Well done!	A Selbstverständlich.
2 Can I take your coat?	B Bitte nehmen Sie Platz.
3 Certainly.	C Gut gemacht!
4 Go on.	D Hätten Sie gern eine Tasse Tee?
5 Please sit down.	E Darf ich Ihnen den Mantel abnehmen?
6 Would you like a cup of tea?	F Nur zu.

C Finish the sentences with the right words.
Vervollständigen Sie die Sätze mit den richtigen Wörtern.

are • has got • have got • is • listen • listens

1 Ewa ____________ a hairdresser.
2 She ____________ a new job.
3 Ewa ____________ to her MP3 player every day.
4 Ewa's parents ____________ jobs in another town.
5 They usually ____________ to the car radio on their way to work.
6 Ewa's parents ____________ very happy about Ewa's new job.

Grammar: have got → G7

I have got	I've got
you have got	you've got
he/she/it has got	he's/she's/it's got
we have got	we've got
you have got	you've got
they have got	they've got

Ziel: Ich kann eine förmliche Email schreiben.

A **Read the text. You do not have to understand every word.**
Lesen Sie den Text. Sie müssen nicht jedes Wort verstehen.

Rules for formal emails

1. Pick a meaningful subject.
2. Start with a polite phrase like "Dear Mrs Taylor".
3. Write in a clear and direct style.
4. Keep it short. Only write what the reader has to know.
5. Avoid jokes and "emoticons".
6. Finish with a polite phrase like "Yours sincerely".
7. Give your full name and company details.
8. Check the email again before you send it.

Now look at the list of topics. Tick the 8 topics that are mentioned in the rules.
Nun schauen Sie sich die Liste der Themen an. Machen Sie ein Häkchen bei den 8 Themen, die in den Regeln erwähnt werden.

- ☐ höfliche Anrede
- ☐ Antwort anhängen
- ☐ aussagekräftiger Betreff
- ☐ richtiges Datum
- ☐ Kontrolle vor Versenden
- ☐ Kopie anfertigen
- ☐ Text kurz halten
- ☐ nie löschen
- ☐ Vor-/Nachname und Firmenadresse angeben
- ☐ klarer Schreibstil
- ☐ höflicher Gruß
- ☐ immer weiterleiten
- ☐ gleichzeitig werben
- ☐ keine Witze/„Emoticons"

B **Read Sammy's email. Why is his boss angry with him?**
Lesen Sie Sammys Email. Warum ist seine Chefin wütend auf ihn?

It's Sammy Tate's first week at ShoeWorld. Today he has to write an email to Ms Khan at another company. This is what the writes:

To:	akhan@newmusic.co...uk
Subject:	Music

Hi
My boss asked me to write this email. Our company, which makes really good shoes, wants to present itself on youTube. My boss thinks that youTube is great for advertising. I think youTube is really cool too. I often watch their videos. We know what we want to show, but we need some music for it. We wondered if your company could help us here. Or are you too busy? ;-))

Bye
Sammy

1 **Mark at least 5 things that are wrong with Sammy's email. Tip: Look at the "Rules for formal emails" above again.**
Markieren Sie mindestens 5 Dinge, die in Sammys Email falsch sind.
Tipp: Sehen Sie sich die „Regeln für förmliche Emails" oben noch einmal an.

2 **Write a new email for Sammy.**
Schreiben Sie eine neue Email für Sammy.

meaningful – aussagekräftig
subject – Betreff
phrase – Redewendung, Ausdruck
clear – klar, deutlich
to avoid – vermeiden
joke – Witz
Yours sincerely – Mit freundlichen Grüßen
company – Firma
details – (Adress-)Daten, Angaben
to ask somebody – jemanden bitten
to present – vorstellen, präsentieren
advertising – Werbung
to wonder – sich fragen

Ziel: Ich kann ein Internet-Formular ausfüllen.

C **Your hobby is hip-hop dancing. You want to order an old DVD from a British internet shop.**
Ihr Hobby ist Hip-Hop Tanz. Sie wollen eine alte DVD bei einem britischen Internet-Shop bestellen.

1 **Read the form. Fill it out with your personal details.**
Lesen Sie das Formular. Füllen Sie es mit Ihren persönlichen Angaben aus.

2 **Note the German words for the field names on the right.**
Notieren Sie rechts die deutschen Begriffe für die Feldnamen.

New customers: Register with brit-film.com first.
Please enter your details.

Title* (Please select:) ○ Mr ○ Ms ○ Mrs
First name* ______
Last name* ______
Email address* ______
Address* ______
City* ______
Postcode* ______
Country* ______
Phone number ______
Password (Minimum 6 characters)* ______
Confirm password* ______
Date of birth ____ DD ____ MM ____ YYYY

*required fields

☐ Please tick this box to receive our newsletter.

Info: In vielen Ländern wird die Postleitzahl auf einer neuen Zeile unter dem Städtenamen genannt.

Feldnamen

Vorname
______
______
______
______
______
______
______
______
______
______

Grammar: There is / There are → G7

There is / There's …	Es ist … / Da ist … / Es gibt …
There are …	Es sind … / Da sind … / Es gibt …

There's a great new video.
Es gibt ein tolles neues Video.

There are lots of people in the club.
Es sind viele Menschen im Club.

D **You tell your friends about the DVD shop. Finish the sentences with *There's* or *There are*.**
Sie erzählen Ihren Freunden von dem DVD Shop. Vervollständigen Sie die Sätze mit *There's* oder *There are*.

1. ______ a great DVD shop online.
2. ______ so many DVDs that I find interesting.
3. ______ lots of internet shops but the others aren't very good.
4. ______ one shop that sells only hip-hop clothes.
5. ______ about 20 hip-hop DVDs in my collection.

to register (with) sich anmelden (bei)
to enter eingeben
title Anrede
to select auswählen
required erforderlich
field Feld
to tick ankreuzen, abhaken
clothes Kleidung
collection Sammlung

I often play football. My brother plays basketball.

Grammar Check 1: *Simple present (I listen to music.)*

Kreuzen Sie die richtige Antwort an. Tragen Sie den Lösungsbuchstaben (nach dem Pfeil) unten auf der Seite ein.

1 Ich benutze das *simple present*, um zu sagen, was ich

- A ☐ letztes Jahr gemacht habe. → B
- B ☐ gerade mache. → R
- C ☒ immer wieder mache. → A

2 Beim *simple present* bleibt das Verb immer gleich, außer bei

- A ☐ I → P
- B ☐ you → N
- C ☐ he/she/it → D

3 In einem Satz mit *simple present* kann als Zeitangabe vorkommen:

- A ☐ right now → R
- B ☐ often → S
- C ☐ yesterday → D

I'm a mechanic. My sister is a gardener.

Grammar Check 2: Das Verb *to be* (= sein)

Kreuzen Sie die richtige Antwort an. Tragen Sie den Lösungsbuchstaben (nach dem Pfeil) unten auf der Seite ein.

4 Die Kurzform *he's* steht für

- A ☐ he is → P
- B ☐ he does → R
- C ☐ he likes → T

5 Die Kurzform von *they are* lautet

- A ☐ there → A
- B ☐ they're → O
- C ☐ their → U

6 Um zu sagen, was jemand von Beruf ist, brauche ich zusätzlich

- A ☐ the → R
- B ☐ one → H
- C ☐ a/an → E

John has got a guitar.

Grammar Check 3: *have got* (= haben, besitzen)

Kreuzen Sie die richtige Antwort an. Tragen Sie den Lösungsbuchstaben (nach dem Pfeil) unten auf der Seite ein.

7 Mit *have got* sage ich, was jemand

- A ☐ ist → R
- B ☐ hat → H
- C ☐ mag → L

8 Nach *he/she/it* benutze ich

- A ☐ have gots → N
- B ☐ has got → E
- C ☐ haves got → T

Grammar Check 4: *There is / There are*

Kreuzen Sie die richtige Antwort an. Tragen Sie den Lösungsbuchstaben (nach dem Pfeil) unten auf der Seite ein.

Look, there's Eminem!!

9 Die Kurzform von *There is* ist

- A ☐ Theirs → N
- B ☐ Ther's → M
- C ☐ There's → H

10 *There are* benutze ich, um über

- A ☐ mehrere → N
- B ☐ vergangene → T
- C ☐ nicht sichtbare → S

Dinge oder Menschen zu sprechen.

Tragen Sie die Lösungsbuchstaben hier ein. Sind alle Fragen richtig beantwortet, ergibt sich ein Wort aus dieser Unit.

9	6	1	2	4	7	5	10	8	3
		A							

Vocabulary Check 1: Verben-Kreuzworträtsel

Tragen Sie die englischen Wörter für die deutschen Verben ein.

Waagerecht →
4 sich anmelden
7 eingeben
9 auswählen
10 vermeiden

Senkrecht ↓
1 bestehen
2 erhalten
3 vorstellen, präsentieren
5 ankreuzen, abhaken
6 trocknen
8 eine SMS schicken, „simsen"

Vocabulary Check 2: Das richtige Wort

Kreuzen Sie jeweils die **drei** richtigen Antworten an. Tragen Sie die Lösungsbuchstaben (nach dem Pfeil) der Reihe nach unten ein.

1 Zeitangaben

A ☐ certainly → J
B ☐ often → H
C ☐ avoid → P
D ☐ usually → A
E ☐ all the time → I

2 Hobbys

A ☐ dance → R
B ☐ cook → D
C ☐ wait → I
D ☐ pass → E
E ☐ read → R

3 Beschreibungen (*Something is …*)

A ☐ curl → A
B ☐ clear → E
C ☐ short → S
D ☐ meaningful → S
E ☐ register → T

4 Feldnamen auf einem Internet-Formular

A ☐ title → E
B ☐ address → R
C ☐ phrase → T
D ☐ password → S
E ☐ collection → D

Lösungswort (Mehrzahl):

☐☐☐ Frage 1 ☐☐☐ Frage 2 ☐☐☐ Frage 3 ☐☐☐ Frage 4

Video lounge

V1 BBC Motion Gallery

Cheerleader auditions

A **Bevor Sie sich das Video ansehen: Was denken Sie, ist Sport bei amerikanischen Studenten sehr beliebt?**

A ☐ Ja. B ☐ Nein.

B **Nach dem Ansehen des Videos: Machen Sie ein Häkchen an die richtige Antwort.**

1 Konnie möchte …

A ☐ Trainerin
B ☐ Cheerleaderin
C ☐ Preisrichterin

werden.

2 Konnie kommt aus Großbritannien. Sie ist zu Gast in …

A ☐ Kanada.
B ☐ Kolumbien.
C ☐ Kalifornien.

A Our free time

Clara and Ivan have got a form. It's about how often they do free time activities. Look at the form and write sentences.

1 Clara always writes messages. Ivan sometimes writes messages.
2 Clara and Ivan often play football.
3 Ivan always repairs things. Clara never repairs things.
4 Clara and Ivan sometimes go swimming.
5 Clara ~~often~~ a often watches films. Ivan sometimes watches films.

	always	often	sometimes	never
1 write messages	Clara	—	Ivan	—
2 play football	—	Clara, Ivan	—	—
3 repair things	Ivan	—	—	Clara
4 go swimming	—	—	Clara, Ivan	—
5 watch films	—	Clara	Ivan	—

B Lauranna

Read Laura's text and fill in the right words.

~~are~~ • ~~he's~~ • ~~I'm~~ • ~~is (3x)~~ • ~~she's~~ • ~~they're~~ • we're • you're

1 My name is Laura. I'm a singer in a pop band.
2 The other band members are really cool. they're my friends.
3 Tom is the band leader. He's a little older than the others.
4 The drummer is my best friend Anna. She's great!
5 we're in the same class at school.
6 Tom always says, "you're like sisters – pop sisters!" So he called our band "Lauranna".

Grammar: he, she, it → G1

Verb	+ -s/-es
cook	cooks
watch	watches
carry	carries

C Emma's new job

Complete the sentences with the simple present. Use the verbs in brackets.

1 Emma has got **[have got]** a new job.
2 She works **[work]** for a big company now.
3 Her customers come **[come]** from lots of countries.
4 But they all speak **[speak]** English.
5 Emma talks **[talk]** all the time.
6 She likes **[like]** her job as a call centre agent.

form
Form; Formular

message
Nachricht, Botschaft

member
Mitglied

drummer
Schlagzeuger/in

call centre agent
Callcenteragent/in

D Call centre rules

Emma knows the rules at the call centre.

1 So she's always polite to the customers.
2 She always talks and smiles.
3 She always uses the customer's name.
4 She never forgets to say "thank you".
5 She never uses negative words.
6 She never talks too long.

When a new call centre agent starts work at the call centre, Emma tells her the rules:

1 Always be polite to ______.
2 Always ______.
3 ______.
4 Never forget ______.
5 ______.
6 ______.

E My hobby

Pick the right word and complete the sentences.

it's • there are • there's • they're

1 there's a halfpipe in the park for skateboarders.
2 So every afternoon theyre in the park with their skateboards.
3 there are about 12 skateboarders in the park every day, boys and girls.
4 they're really good at skateboarding.
5 it's fun to go and watch them.
6 it's my hobby!

F Jack the rapper

Put the phrases in the right order and make sentences.

1 really loves | my friend Jack | rap music
my friend Jack really loves rap music.
2 to it on his | MP3 player every day | he listens
He listens to it on his Mp3.
3 from an internet company | posters of rappers | he often buys
He often buys posters of rappers.
4 goes to Germany | every summer Jack | for a big rap festival
every Summer Jack goes to Germany for a.
5 meets lots of | friends there | he always
He always meets lots of friends there.

Textarbeit: Questions on the text

A1.21

Poor in a rich country

Millions of Americans need help to feed themselves

In a rich country more and more people are becoming poor. In large areas of the USA, for example in states like Ohio or Michigan, thousands of people had jobs making cars, fridges or other goods. But a few years ago their companies closed down and started to produce goods in Asia, where work is cheaper.

Who are the poor in America? A family of two adults and two children with less than $20,500 a year is called poor. This means that about 36.5 million Americans are poor today! About 8% of white people are called poor and 24% of black people.

Of course, the government helps. People with low incomes can get food stamps. $33 billion was spent last year and helped about 26 million people. But the government only gives up to $3 per person per day in food stamps – and that is not enough today because prices for food or energy to heat your home are going up.

That is why many people who do not know how to feed themselves go to food banks or soup kitchens. In New York alone 1.3 million people use these services. Jim Brenizer, organizer of a food bank says: "Years ago we did a lot of work for old people who had little or no money but today we are helping more and more people that don't earn enough money – 'the working poor'. A growing problem for us is that supermarkets and hotels are managing their food better today so there is less food left over that we can give to poor people."

(276 words)

Annotations:
headline **to feed (themselves)** – (sich) ernähren
line 10 **adult** – Erwachsene/r
line 15 **government** – Regierung
line 16 **food stamps** – Essensmarken
line 24 **food bank** – Ausgabestelle für kostenlose Nahrungsmittel

Skills Tip: Die *Questions on the text* müssen in ganzen Sätzen beantwortet werden.

- Lesen Sie den Text einmal ganz durch. Schauen Sie sich das Foto an. Worum geht es?
- Lesen Sie den Text noch einmal gründlich durch. Bleiben Sie ruhig, wenn Sie ein Wort nicht verstehen. Überlegen Sie: Was könnte das Wort in diesem Zusammenhang bedeuten? Kennen Sie ein ähnliches Wort?
- Nun lesen Sie die **Arbeitsanweisungen** gründlich.
- Achten Sie auf **Fragewörter** (z. B. *who, when, where*) und auf die **Zeit**, in der die Frage gestellt ist (*past, present, future*).
- **Wichtig:** Sie dürfen Teile der Frage oder Teile vom Text wörtlich für Ihre Antwort benutzen!
- Meistens gibt es 4 Schreibzeilen für jede Antwort. Sie müssen nicht alle ausfüllen.

Answer in complete English sentences, please.

1 Name two things which companies in Michigan or Ohio **produced** some years ago.

___

2 **How does** the government help the poor?

___

___

3 Name two places where poor people **can** also get help.

___

Managing Situations: Talking to people – Complete the dialogue

Skills Tip: *Talking to people* ist eine Zuordnungsübung.

- Lesen Sie gründlich die **Situationsbeschreibung** über dem Dialog und alle Aussagen.
- Die **erste Antwort** ist bereits eingetragen.
- Achten Sie auf **Wortwiederholungen** in Frage und Antwort.
- Stellen Sie fest, welche Fragen mit **Yes/No** beantwortet werden können und suchen Sie nach solchen Satzanfängen.
- **Wichtig:** Zwei der Sätze rechts (A – I) passen gar nicht!

You work as a hairdresser. A customer, Ms Hill, comes into the salon.
Match the sentences to complete the dialogue. Two phrases do not match.

YOU

[D] 1 Good morning, Ms Hill. Have you got an appointment?

[ ] 2 You're lucky. There has been a cancellation *(Absage)*.

[ ] 3 Please sit down. What can I do for you today, Ms Hill?

[ ] 4 No problem. **Did you have** a special style in mind?

[ ] 5 Certainly, Ms Hill. Like **last time**?

[ ] 6 I'm glad to hear that. **Would you like** a cup of tea or coffee?

[ ] 7 **Would you like** your hair **washed**?

8 OK, I won't use shampoo then.

A CUSTOMER (Ms Hill)

A **No, not really.** I thought perhaps you could curl my hair again.

B **No, thanks.** I'm fine.

C I think you're right. Thank you.

D **No, I haven't. Sorry. I thought perhaps it would be OK?**

E Well, I have to look really good tonight!

F That's great! Thank you.

G **No, thanks.** I **washed** it yesterday.

H Yes, the curls that you did **last time** looked really good.

I That really is a good price.

45j9ub

2 In touch

Ziel: Ich kann fragen/sagen, was gewöhnlich (nicht) der Fall ist.
Beispiel: Does he listen to music? Yes, he does. / No, he doesn't. (simple present)

A Why does Yasmin ask Hamit so many questions?
Warum stellt Yasmin Hamit so viele Fragen?

Yasmin is a junior reporter. Today she has to write to famous football player Hamit and ask him some questions.

Yasmin

Yasmin's questions — Hamit's answers

1. Do you use social networks?
Yes, I do. I've got millions of friends out there!

2. Do you write lots of emails?
No, I don't. I just haven't got the time.

3. Does your mobile often ring?
Yes, it does. It's terrible.

4. Does your girlfriend usually send you emails?
No, she doesn't. She rings me!

Hamit

1 What do you think? Does Yasmin want to write about Hamit's last football match?

☐ Yes, she does. ☐ No, she doesn't.

2 Does Hamit really know millions of people?

☐ Yes, he does. ☐ No, he doesn't.

Vocabulary: Kommunikation im Netz

blog, chat, community, download, email, mail, online, post, profile, (web)site, skype, social network

in touch – in Verbindung
junior reporter – Nachwuchs-reporter/in
social network – soziales Netzwerk
football match – Fußballspiel
community – Gemeinschaft
to post something – etwas ins Internet stellen
profile – Profil, Selbstdarstellung

Grammar: Fragen, was gewöhnlich der Fall ist → G1

Do I work?	Do you sometimes read my blog?
Do you work?	Liest du manchmal mein Blog?
Does he/she/it work?	Does Mel often surf the internet?
Do we work?	Surft Mel oft im Internet?
Do you work?	Do your friends like texting?
Do they work?	Schicken deine Freunde gern SMS?

B What about you?
Und Sie?

1 Do you use social networks?

☐ Yes, I do. ☐ No, I don't.

2 Does your mobile often ring?

☐ Yes, it does. ☐ No, it doesn't.

Terrible Tom

A **Listen to the story. Tick the right picture (1–3).**
A1.3 Hören Sie sich die Geschichte an. Machen Sie ein Häkchen an das passende Bild (1–3).

1 
2 
3 

B **Listen to the story again. Tick A or B for sentences 1–4.**
Hören Sie sich die Geschichte noch einmal an. Machen Sie bei den Sätzen 1–4 ein Häkchen bei A oder B.

1 A ☐ Patty and Tom are neighbours.
B ☐ Patty phones Tom.

2 A ☐ Melinda is a customer.
B ☐ It's Melinda's birthday.

3 A ☐ The colleagues meet in the canteen.
B ☐ Melinda doesn't like her present.

4 A ☐ Tom sells cars.
B ☐ Melinda has got a birthday cake.

Grammar: **Etwas nicht tun oder sein** → G1+7

I don't work	I'm not terrible
you don't work	you aren't terrible
he/she/it doesn't work	he/she/it isn't terrible
we don't work	we aren't terrible
you don't work	you aren't terrible
they don't work	they aren't terrible

Vocabulary:
Freunde und Bekannte
- friend, boyfriend, girlfriend, partner
- neighbour, classmate
- colleague, customer, boss

C **Who is Jens? Choose the correct word and fill it in.**
Wer ist Jens? Suchen Sie das richtige Wort aus und tragen Sie es ein.

Example: Jens ______________ [is / does] one of Tom's friends. → *Jens is one of Tom's friends.*

1 ______________ [Does / Is] Jens work at Barker's Garage too?
2 No, he ______________ [doesn't / isn't].
3 ______________ [Do / Are] Tom and Jens often go out together?
4 No, they ______________ [aren't / don't].
5 Tom ______________ [doesn't / isn't] really know Jens.
6 Tom and Jens ______________ [are / do] only social network friends!

Grammar: **Fragen, was jemand ist oder hat** → G7

Is she English?	Ist sie Engländerin?
Are your friends nice?	Sind deine Freunde nett?
Have you got a social network profile?	Hast du eine Profilseite in einem sozialen Netzwerk?
Has Emma got a new mobile?	Hat Emma ein neues Handy?

neighbour Nachbar/in
colleague Kollege/Kollegin
canteen Kantine
boyfriend/ girlfriend (feste/r) Freund/in
classmate Klassen-kamerad/in

FamousMeBook

A1.4 Here's an internet ad.

FamousMeBook

- Does your busy life make it difficult for you to stay in touch with your friends?
- Do you want to make interesting new friends all over the world?
- Do you want to share your thoughts, your feelings and your photos with everybody?

If your answer to these questions is "Yes", we offer you **VIP membership** of the world's coolest online community – FamousMeBook.

Register today and meet **V**ery **I**nteresting **P**eople!

Julia likes the FamousMeBook ad. She's skyping her friend Ronnie in England.

Julia: Hi, Ronnie. Everything OK?
Ronnie: Don't ask. How are things with you, Julia? Are you back in Germany now?
Julia: Yes, I am, unfortunately. Listen, Ronnie, do you know FamousMeBook?
Ronnie: Yes, I do! Unfortunately!
Julia: What do you mean?
Ronnie: Well … Do you remember that job interview that I told you about?
Julia: Yes, of course. When is it again? Next week?
Ronnie: That's right. But I don't think that I want to go there now.
Julia: Are you crazy? You said that Dupont's is the classiest restaurant in town.
Ronnie: Yeah, and the classiest people in town go there. Real VIPs, do you understand? **V**ery **I**mportant **P**eople, not **V**ery **I**diotic **P**eople, like people who use FamousMeBook!

Julia: Stop, stop, stop! What's the problem?
Ronnie: OK. Do you remember Saturday?
Julia: Do you mean Jill's party? Of course I do. It was fun. Everybody drank too much.
Ronnie: Yes, everybody, including me. And then I put some CDs in the oven.
Julia: Yes, there was smoke everywhere! I took a photo of you with your mobile.
Ronnie: Yeah, thanks for that. Do you know what I did with the photo when I came home late at night? I posted it on FamousMeBook. All my "friends" thought it was very funny – except Monsieur Pierre Dupont. He phoned me and told me that in his restaurant they put food in ovens, not CDs.
Julia: Oh dear!
Ronnie: And then he said, "Also, for reasons of hygiene, working in your underwear is not allowed at Dupont's!" Do you understand that I don't really want to go there any more next week?

Vocabulary: denken, fühlen usw.

feel, know, like, love, mean, remember, think, understand, want

ad Anzeige
to make friends Freundschaften schließen
all over the world überall auf der Welt
to share teilen
thought Gedanke
feeling Gefühl
membership Mitgliedschaft
unfortunately leider
job interview Vorstellungsgespräch
crazy verrückt
classy edel, elegant
real echt, wirklich
idiotic idiotisch
including einschließlich
oven Backofen
reasons of hygiene hygienische Gründe

A EXAM **Are these statements true or false? Write your answer after the statement.**
Sind diese Aussagen richtig oder falsch? Schreiben Sie Ihre Antwort hinter die Aussage.

Skills Tip

Lesen Sie sich die Aussage gut durch. Dann entscheiden Sie, ob die Aussage richtig oder falsch ist. Überprüfen Sie Ihre Entscheidung, indem Sie Sätze mit „stimmt" (= richtig) oder „stimmt nicht" (= falsch) formulieren, z. B.: „Es stimmt nicht, dass die Internet-Anzeige für einen Online-Shop wirbt".

	Aussage	richtig oder falsch?
1	Die Internet-Anzeige wirbt für einen Online-Shop.	falsch
2	Ronnies Vorstellungsgespräch ist in der nächsten Woche.	________
3	Julia war am Samstag auch auf Jills Party.	________
4	Ronnie legte zwei CDs in den Backofen.	________
5	Ronnie löschte das Foto von der Party aus Versehen.	________

B EXAM **Find the right word for definitions 1–5.**
Finden Sie zu den Worterklärungen 1–5 das passende Wort.

Skills Tip

Die gesuchten Wörter kommen alle im Text links vor. Wenn Sie unsicher sind, schauen Sie dort noch einmal nach, ob Ihnen der Zusammenhang hilft.

community • food • restaurant • ~~thought~~ • underwear

1 Something that you think: thought
2 A group of people: ________
3 A place where you can buy and eat a meal: ________
4 What you eat: ________
5 Clothes that you wear under other clothes: ________

C **Circle the right phrase.**
Umkringeln Sie den richtigen Ausdruck.

Example:
→ *My friend* *hasn't got* / *haven't got* *a social network profile.*

1 She thinks that social networks aren't / isn't a good idea.
2 I doesn't / don't agree with her.
3 What do / does you think about social networks?
4 Have you got / Has you got hundreds of friends too?

Grammar: have not got → G 7

I haven't got
you haven't got
he/she/it hasn't got
we haven't got
you haven't got
they haven't got

to agree
zustimmen

Ziel: Ich kann mich vorstellen.

New at work

A1.5 Alex has gone abroad. He works as a machine operator at Newtec in Birmingham. He likes to go to the firm's canteen in his lunch break. One day he sees a nice young woman there.

Alex	Hi. Do you mind if I sit here?
Vanessa	No, I don't. Go ahead.
Alex	Thanks. My name is Alex, by the way.
Vanessa	And I'm Vanessa. Nice to meet you, Alex. Are you new here?
Alex	Yes, I am. I work in Production. And you?
Vanessa	I'm a management assistant. I started to work here almost two years ago.
Alex	And do you like it here?
Vanessa	Yes, I do. My boss is usually friendly and the pay isn't bad. What about you?
Alex	Oh, I don't know yet. I've only just started. I like the canteen!
Vanessa	Yes, it's OK. So see you again tomorrow perhaps?
Alex	Great idea. See you for lunch tomorrow.

A EXAM **Match questions 1 – 6 with answers A – F. Draw lines.**
Ordnen Sie die Fragen 1 – 6 den Antworten A – F zu. Ziehen Sie Linien.

1 What's your name?
2 How old are you?
3 What's your job?
4 Where do you work?
5 Do you like it here?
6 See you again tomorrow perhaps?

A I'm a machine operator.
B I like the canteen!
C My name is Alex.
D Yes, see you tomorrow.
E I'm 20.
F I work in Production.

B Choose exercise 1 or 2.
Wählen Sie Aufgabe 1 oder 2.

1 Complete Alex' email to his friend. If you need help, read the dialogue above again.
Vervollständigen Sie Alex' Email an seinen Freund. Wenn Sie Hilfe brauchen, lesen Sie den Dialog oben noch einmal.

I talked to one of my new colleagues today. Her name is ________________ [1] and she's really nice. She works as a ________________________________ [2] in my new firm. She started to work there ________ [3] years ago. Vanessa likes the firm. She says her ________________ [4] is usually friendly and she thinks the pay is OK. I'm going to see her again for ________________ [5] tomorrow!

2 A few days later Alex talks to John, who works as an electrician in the same firm. Write a similar dialogue to the one above.
Ein paar Tage später unterhält sich Alex mit John, der als Elektriker in derselben Firma arbeitet. Schreiben Sie einen ähnlichen Dialog wie den oben.

abroad
im/ins Ausland

machine operator
Maschinenführer/in

firm
Firma

lunch break
Mittagspause

to mind
etwas dagegen haben

Go ahead.
Mach nur. / Machen Sie nur.

by the way
übrigens

production
Produktion

management assistant
Bürokauffrau/-mann

pay
Bezahlung, Gehalt

not yet
noch nicht

perhaps
vielleicht

Ziel: Ich kann für ein soziales Netzwerk ein Profil von mir anfertigen.

C **Read the four profiles. Then read the information 1–4 below. Put the right name under each profile.**
Lesen Sie die vier Profile. Dann lesen Sie die Informationen 1–4 darunter. Schreiben Sie den richtigen Namen unter jedes Profil.

Wall | Info | Photos | Links | Video

About me · Basic info

Gender	male	female	male	female
Birthday	25 May 1991	4 March 1989	9 June 1993	25 April 1992
Brothers/Sisters	Ben	---	Nazan	Daniel, Lukas
Relationship Status	single	in a relationship	single	single
Interested in	women	women	women	men
Looking for	a relationship	friendship	dating	friendship
Current Location	Wiesbaden	London	Hamburg	Wiesbaden
Political Views	green	liberal	green	---
Name				

1 Jessica is interested in women. She's looking for friendship. She doesn't live in Wiesbaden.

2 Suat hasn't got a girlfriend. His political views are green. He has got one sister.

3 Anna is looking for friendship. She lives in Wiesbaden. She doesn't tell us her political views.

4 Axel isn't in a relationship. His birthday is on the 25th. He has got one brother.

Grammar: mein, dein, usw. → G13

my	**Die Formen bleiben immer gleich:**
your	
his/her/its	**That's her profile.** Das ist ihr Profil.
our	**I don't like her music.** Mir gefällt ihre Musik nicht.
your	
their	**Tim and Tom are her brothers.** Tim und Tom sind ihre Brüder.

D EXAM **Fill in the correct English words. Tip: They are all in the Grammar Box above.**
Tragen Sie die richtigen englischen Wörter ein. Tipp: Die Wörter stehen alle im *Grammar*-Kasten oben.

1 Mark is my boyfriend. ____________ [seine] favourite music is techno.

2 We often go to clubs together. We meet ____________ [unsere] friends there.

3 ____________ [meine] mother says I should stay at home more often.

4 But my father says, "It's ____________ [dein] life now. You can do what you like."

5 My friends have more problems at home. ____________ [ihre] parents are more difficult.

6 My friend Aylin doesn't even have a social network profile. ____________ [ihre] mother doesn't allow it.

wall
(Pinn-)Wand

basic info
allgemeine Informationen

gender
Geschlecht

male/female
männlich/weiblich

relationship
Beziehung

status
Status

interested in
interessiert an

looking for
auf der Suche nach

friendship
Freundschaft

current location
derzeitiger Wohnort

political views
politische Einstellung

to allow
erlauben

Grammar Check 1: Fragen im *simple present*

Kreuzen Sie die richtige Antwort an. Tragen Sie den Lösungsbuchstaben (nach dem Pfeil) unten auf der Seite ein.

1 Mit Fragen im *simple present* frage ich danach, was

A ☒ gewöhnlich der Fall ist. → R
B ☐ in diesem Moment passiert. → L
C ☐ gestern der Fall war. → T

2 Für Fragen im *simple present* brauche ich

A ☐ make/makes → R
B ☐ be → S
C ☐ do/does → N

3 *Does* benutze ich mit

A ☐ I/you → T
B ☐ he/she/it → H
C ☐ we/they/you → L

Grammar Check 2: Verneinungen

Kreuzen Sie die richtige Antwort an. Tragen Sie den Lösungsbuchstaben (nach dem Pfeil) unten auf der Seite ein.

I really don't know. I haven't got an idea.

4 Die Kurzform von *do not* ist

A ☐ don't → D
B ☐ aren't → T
C ☐ doesn't → N

5 Die Kurzform *isn't* steht für

A ☐ has not → I
B ☐ is not → E
C ☐ does not → A

6 Die Verneinung von *I've got* ist

A ☐ I don't have got → O
B ☐ I haven't got → I
C ☐ I've gotn't → E

Grammar Check 3: Besitz angeben

Kreuzen Sie die richtige Antwort an. Tragen Sie den Lösungsbuchstaben (nach dem Pfeil) unten auf der Seite ein.

Luiz with his motorbike.

7 Um zu sagen, wem etwas gehört, benutze ich Wörter wie

A ☐ my, his, our → S
B ☐ he, she, it → C
C ☐ and, or, but → T

8 Um zu sagen, das etwas mir gehört, benutze ich

A ☐ your → E
B ☐ her → A
C ☐ my → I

9 Um zu sagen, dass etwas ihnen (z. B. den Kindern) gehört, benutze ich

A ☐ there → C
B ☐ their → F
C ☐ they're → P

10 Mein Motorrad oder meine Motorräder – die Form von *my*

A ☐ bleibt gleich. → P
B ☐ verändert sich. → B

Tragen Sie die Lösungsbuchstaben hier ein. Sind alle Fragen richtig beantwortet, ergibt sich ein Wort aus dieser Unit.

9	1	8	5	2	4	7	3	6	10
	R								

Vocabulary Check 1: Suchworträtsel

Finden Sie 12 neue Wörter aus dieser Unit. Die Definitionen rechts neben dem Rätsel können Ihnen helfen.

M	U	P	C	P	F	B	E	L	S	B	C	I	W	P	A	Y
O	G	W	A	L	L	R	R	E	P	O	R	T	E	R	P	E
K	S	E	N	A	W	E	N	V	I	Y	A	S	M	O	N	D
A	C	I	T	X	U	G	D	C	W	F	C	A	N	F	R	A
L	R	N	E	I	G	H	B	O	U	R	H	F	F	I	R	M
L	Y	S	E	M	N	T	A	L	B	I	M	P	C	L	G	H
O	V	E	N	L	I	C	O	L	L	E	A	G	U	E	R	S
W	A	N	R	U	V	L	T	H	T	N	D	R	S	V	A	R
P	R	O	C	B	E	L	E	G	I	D	I	O	T	I	C	B

Waagerecht →
- Backofen
- Bezahlung, Gehalt
- Firma
- idiotisch
- Kollege/Kollegin
- Nachbar/in
- (Pinn-)Wand
- Reporter/in

Senkrecht ↓
- erlauben
- (fester) Freund
- Kantine
- Profil, Selbstdarstellung

Vocabulary Check 2: Gegensätze und Synonyme

Kreuzen Sie die richtige Antwort an. Tragen Sie den Lösungsbuchstaben (nach dem Pfeil) unten ein.

1 Was ist der Gegensatz von *easy*?
- A ☐ idiotic → S
- B ☐ classy → T
- C ☐ difficult → R

2 Was ist der Gegensatz von *funny*?
- A ☐ sad → E
- B ☐ short → A
- C ☐ crazy → I

3 Was ist der Gegensatz von *buy*?
- A ☐ mind → S
- B ☐ share → T
- C ☐ sell → P

4 Was ist ein Synonym (Wort mit gleicher oder ähnlicher Bedeutung) für *begin*?
- A ☐ allow → U
- B ☐ start → A
- C ☐ status → I

5 Was ist ein Synonym (Wort mit gleicher oder ähnlicher Bedeutung) für *company*?
- A ☐ firm → P
- B ☐ field → T
- C ☐ female → B

Lösungswort:

5	2	1		4	3	
			H			S

Video lounge

◎ V2 BBC Motion Gallery

Making music

Machen Sie ein Häkchen an die richtigen Antworten.

1 Im Video geht es darum, …
- A ☐ wie man eine Band gründet.
- B ☐ wie ein Song entsteht.

2 Wir sehen …
- A ☐ einen Produzenten und eine Sängerin.
- B ☐ eine Bandleaderin und einen Sänger.

A The new job

It's your first day at your new job. You've got a nice colleague – and lots of questions for her. Make the questions.

Wie fragen Sie die Kollegin, …

1 ob sie viele Emails schreibt? ______________________________?

2 ob das Telefon oft klingelt *(ring)*? ______________________________?

3 wann sie gewöhnlich *(usually)* nach Hause geht? *When* ______________________________

______________________________?

4 ob es ihr hier gefällt? ______________________________?

B The wrong person

Sophie is a call centre agent. Her job is to phone people and ask them questions. But she has always got the wrong person on the phone. Write the person's answers.

Example:
→ *"Now, Mrs Miller, you live in London …" – "No, I don't live in London!"*

1 "Now, Mr Parker, you drive a Ford …"

– "No, ______________________________!"

2 "Now, Mrs Singer, you're a hairdresser …"

– "No, ______________________________!"

3 "Now, Mr Fox, you've got a motorbike …"

– "No, ______________________________!"

4 "Now, Mrs Bell, your partner works for KM …"

– "No, ______________________________!"

5 "Now, Mr Lang, your hobby is reading …"

– "No, ______________________________!"

C The job interview

EXAM Match the questions 1–5 to the short answers A–F. Draw lines. One answer does not match.

1 Do you like talking on the phone?	A Yes, I have.
2 Have you got your own car?	B No, it isn't.
3 Are you good at French?	C Yes, she is.
4 Does your boss know that you're here?	D Yes, I do.
5 Is your job interesting?	E No, I'm not.
	F No, she doesn't.

motorbike
Motorrad

own
eigene/r/s

French
Französisch

Grammar: Kurzantworten → G1+7

Do you …?	– Yes, I do. / No, I don't.
Is she …?	– Yes, she is. / No, she isn't.
Have they got …?	– Yes, they have. / No, they haven't.

D My birthday photo

Complete the text with the right pronouns (my, your, etc.).

I love this photo. I took it on my birthday. On the left you can see ______________ [1] best friend Lola. ______________ [2] birthday is two days after my birthday. She always says, "My hair is so boring, but I love ______________ [3] hair!" Next to her is my brother. ______________ [4] name is Luke. He always asks Lola and me very stupid questions like "What's ______________ [5] favourite number?" In the middle, that's me, of course. And the two people on the right are my colleagues, Tim and Sue. We haven't got the same boss. ______________ [6] boss is much nicer than my boss! We often go to the "Lion's Head" after work. We all agree that it's ______________ [7] favourite pub.

E Definitions

Pick the right word for definitions 1–5.

colleague • classmate • customer • firm • friendship • gender • neighbour • pub • status

1. A person that you work with: ______________________________
2. A place where people go to drink and meet their friends: ______________________________
3. A person who buys something from a shop: ______________________________
4. A relationship between friends: ______________________________
5. A person who lives next to you: ______________________________

F Mike's job

Complete the sentences with the words in brackets.

1. Mike has got a ______________ but he ______________ the ______________ job. **[hasn't got / job / right]**
2. He's good ______________ talking ______________ people, but he isn't good ______________. **[at / enough / to]**
3. He ______________ French but he doesn't ______________ it ______________ enough. **[fast / speak / speaks]**
4. He knows the ______________ but he doesn't know ______________ about ______________. **[computers / internet / much]**
5. He asks himself: "______________ I really ______________ stay in a job that ______________ right for me?" **[do / isn't / want to]**

to take a photo ein Foto machen
on the left links
next to neben
to agree sich einig sein
pub Kneipe
between zwischen
enough genug

Textarbeit: Finish the sentences

A1.22

eBay

Everyone knows it. Millions of people in Great Britain or Germany use it. Private users sell books, old mobile phones, car parts or other things that they do not need any more. Companies also sell their products on eBay.

So eBay has become big business. But it is more than just a business name – it has made the internet into a worldwide marketplace for new and used goods.

The only thing it needs is millions of people. "I like the idea that somebody can use the things that I do not need any more," says 18-year-old Anna Smith from Durham. "Today we throw away too many things although they are not broken. And I can even earn a little money in this way. My grandparents bought me a new mobile phone for Christmas which is better than my old one. That's why I sold my old mobile on eBay. That was really good fun!"

It all started in 1995 when Pierre Omidyar, a French student who lived in Silicon Valley in the USA, made a website on which he offered an old printer for sale. Somebody gave him $15 for it and a new internet business was born. Later Omidyar called it eBay. As we all know, this idea has become very successful.

Even such a great idea also has its negative sides. Some people offer useless goods at high prices. Some just take the money and do not send the goods to the buyer. Criminals steal credit card numbers and eBay passwords on the internet. "You have to be careful," says Anna, "but it really is a good thing!" (269 words)

Annotations:
line 3 **user** – Benutzer/in, Nutzer/in
line 16 **although** – obwohl
line 25 **to offer for sale** – zum Verkauf anbieten
line 29 **successful** – erfolgreich

Skills Tip: In *Finish the sentences* müssen Sie Sätze zu Ende führen.

- Lesen Sie zuerst den Text gründlich.
- Dann lesen Sie die erste Satzhälfte.
- Achten Sie besonders darauf, mit welchen Worten **diese Satzhälfte aufhört** (z. B. *because, so, but* und *he, she* etc.). Machen Sie sich klar, was danach erwartet wird.
- **Wichtig:** Sie dürfen Teile vom Text wörtlich für Ihre Antwort benutzen! Aber meistens müssen Sie den Text etwas ändern, damit er zum Satzanfang passt.

Use **only** information from the text, please.

1 Pierre Omidyar wanted to sell a printer **so he ...**

____

2 Anna Smith got a new mobile phone **and then she ...**

____

3 eBay is very successful **because ...**

____

4 Anna knows that the internet is dangerous **so she ...**

____

Managing Situations: Talking to people – Complete the dialogue

Skills Tip: Die Zuordnungen bei *Talking to people* müssen auch logisch passen.

- Lesen Sie jede Aussage gründlich. Der **2. Satz** einer Aussage kann entscheidend sein.
- Beachten Sie jedes Wort. Manchmal geben **kleine Wörter** wichtige Hinweise.
- Prüfen Sie nach jeder Zuordnung, ob auch die nächste Reaktion des Gesprächspartners passt.
- **Denken Sie daran:** Zwei der Sätze rechts (A – I) passen gar nicht!

You have got a new job. In your lunch break you meet a nice colleague in the canteen.
Match the sentences to complete the dialogue. Two phrases do not match.

YOU

[E] 1 Hi. **Do you mind if I sit here?**

[ ] 2 Thanks. My name is ..., by the way.

[ ] 3 Nice to meet you **too**, Murat.

[ ] 4 Yes, I am. I work in Production. And you?

[ ] 5 And do you like it here?

[ ] 6 Oh, I don't know yet. I like the canteen!

[ ] 7 OK. I love pizza!

8 Great idea. See you for lunch tomorrow.

A COLLEAGUE

A No, I don't. **I'm an electrician.**
B Yes, I do. It's interesting. What about you?
C Me too. See you again tomorrow perhaps?
D I'm 20. And you?
E No, I don't. **Go ahead.**
F Yes, it's OK. You have to try the pizza here. It's great.
G And I'm Murat. Nice to meet you.
H I'm an electrician. I started to work here almost two years ago.
I Are you new here?

3 A place of my own

Ziel: Ich kann sagen, was ich gerade mache. *Beispiel: I'm reading. (present progressive)*

A **What are Rana and Sam doing at the moment? Read the text messages.**
Was machen Rana und Sam im Moment? Lesen Sie die SMS-Nachrichten.

1 **Who do you think has got his/her own place?**

____

2 **And who is still living with his/her parents?**

____

Vocabulary: **Was man im Alltag tut**

check emails, clean, cook, do the washing, iron, listen to music, make the bed, play games, phone friends, read, surf the internet, wash the dishes, watch TV

Grammar: **Was jemand gerade tut** → G 2

I am	I'm	…ing
you are	you're	
he/she/it is	he's/she's/it's	
we are	we're	
you are	you're	
they are	they're	

Right now, I'm reading.
Im Augenblick lese ich.

Dan is watching TV at the moment.
Dan sieht gerade fern.

My parents are cooking now.
Meine Eltern kochen jetzt.

B **It's 9 o'clock on Sunday evening. What are Rana and Sam doing now? What do you think?**
Es ist Sonntagabend, 9 Uhr. Was machen Rana und Sam jetzt? Was meinen Sie?

I think Rana is ______________________________

I think Sam is ______________________________

a place of my own
meine eigene Bleibe

right now
im Augenblick

just
gerade, soeben

to do the washing
die Wäsche machen

meal
Essen, Mahlzeit

still
immer noch

to iron
bügeln

to wash the dishes
abwaschen, spülen

The pizza problem

A **Listen to the dialogue. Tick the right picture (1–3).**
A1.6 Hören Sie sich den Dialog an. Machen Sie ein Häkchen an das passende Bild (1–3).

1

2

3

B **Listen to the dialogue again. Tick A, B or C for sentences 1–4.**
Hören Sie sich den Dialog noch einmal an. Machen Sie bei den Sätzen 1–4 ein Häkchen bei A, B oder C.

1 Tina is making
A ☐ breakfast.
B ☐ a salad.
C ☐ a sandwich.

2 Paul is doing
A ☐ the lasagne.
B ☐ the pizzas.
C ☐ the washing.

3 At the moment, Tina is working in
A ☐ the sports department.
B ☐ the music department.
C ☐ the food department.

4 Tina is checking
A ☐ Paul.
B ☐ the oven.
C ☐ the packet.

Grammar: Die -ing-Form → G 2

Verb + -ing
cook → cooking
cut → cutting
make → making

C **And what are Tina's neighbours doing? Put in *is* or *are* and the verb in the -ing form.**
Und was machen Tinas Nachbarn? Fügen Sie *is* oder *are* und das Verb in der *-ing*-Form ein.

Example:
Ms Rivera from upstairs ______________ [cut] some carrots.
→ *Ms Rivera from upstairs is cutting some carrots.*

1 Her partner ______________ [**make**] tea.
2 Ben ______________ [**take**] some cookies out of the oven in the flat downstairs.
3 Lisa, his girlfriend, ______________ [**wash**] the dishes.
4 May and Lee are on the same floor as Tina. They aren't cooking, they ______________ [**eat**].

Grammar: Was jemand gerade nicht tut → G 2

I'm not watching TV at the moment.
Ich sehe gerade nicht fern.
Right now, Sue isn't ironing.
Im Augenblick bügelt Sue nicht.

salad
Salat

upstairs/ downstairs
oben/unten (im Haus)

carrot
Möhre, Karotte

flat
Wohnung

floor
Etage, Stockwerk

Flat hunting

A1.7 Tracy and Denzil are looking for a flat. They are reading these adverts online:

FLATHUNTER

Modern flat, kitchen, living room, bathroom, bedroom. Cable TV. Broadband internet. Fully furnished – tables, bed, chairs, sofa – everything! Only £500 per month.

→ Phone 543769, "Matt's Flats", Mr Shrekly

Are you looking for a flat? Widow has got big, old house with garden and wants to share both with nice young people. Only £350 per month.

→ Phone 4578, Mrs Still

Which flat is more interesting for Tracy and Denzil? Find out if you were right.
Welche Wohnung ist interessanter für Tracy und Denzil? Finden Sie heraus, ob Sie Recht hatten?

It's Saturday. Tracy and Denzil are driving to see a flat.

Denzil: Let's hope it's nice.
Tracy: I'm sure it's better than the other flat. The other flat is old, and I bet the woman who lives there is as old as the house!
Denzil: Yes, and I'm sure she has got lots of jobs for us, that garden, for example.
Tracy: And in the evenings when you're trying to read …
Denzil: … the old woman is watching her terrible TV shows. – Look, we're here. I like the colour of the building.

15 minutes later …

Denzil: Let's drive away – fast!
Tracy: Yes. I'm still shaking. That terrible furniture! And the awful smell. Uggh!
Denzil: I'm sure there are rats in the building. This must be the worst flat in England.
Tracy: Forget Mr Shrekly's flat. We aren't moving out! We're staying at my parents' house.

At the same time Mrs Still is talking to her new partner.

Mrs Still: Hello, Lou. It's so sad. Nobody is interested in my wonderful flat.
Lou: Too bad. All that new furniture, cable TV, broadband. And it's so big! Ah well, the garden is waiting for me …
Mrs Still: Can we look at the advert again first?
Lou: Yes, I think we should change it. You have to find somebody soon. This house is too expensive for you.

Vocabulary: In der Wohnung (Nomen)

- bathroom, bedroom, kitchen, living room
- bed, chair, cupboard, shelf, sofa, table
- cable TV, broadband

flat hunting Wohnungssuche
advert Anzeige
cable TV Kabelfernsehen
broadband Breitband
furnished möbliert
widow Witwe
to bet wetten
as old as so alt wie
to shake zittern
furniture Möbel
awful furchtbar
smell Geruch
rat Ratte
the worst flat die schlimmste Wohnung
to move out ausziehen
Too bad. Schade.
cupboard Schrank
shelf, shelves Regal, Regale

A EXAM **Questions on the text. Answer the questions.**
Fragen zum Text. Beantworten Sie die Fragen.

Skills Tip

Meistens sind die Fragen in der Reihenfolge des Textes aufgeschrieben, das heißt die Antwort auf die erste Frage findet sich eher oben im Text, die Antwort auf die letzte Frage eher unten usw.

1 How much does the modern flat cost per month? 500€
2 Who likes the colour of the building? Denzil
3 Where do Tracy and Denzil want to stay now? ______
4 What do Mrs Still and Lou want to change? ______

B EXAM **Match the sentence parts. Draw lines.**
Ordnen Sie die Satzhälften einander zu. Ziehen Sie Linien.

1 The name of the "modern" building is …
2 Denzil: Mr Shrekly's flat …
3 Tracy: The smell of the flat was …
4 Her parents' house is …
5 In the old house, the furniture of the flat …
6 Mrs Still's partner is …

A awful!
B big enough for them all.
C helping her with the garden.
D is the worst flat in England!
E not "Matt's Rats"!
F is new.

Grammar: Wessen? → G14

Tracy's car	my parents' place	the colour of the building
Tracys Auto	das Haus meiner Eltern	die Farbe des Gebäudes
(= eine Person)	(= mehrere Personen)	(= Sachen)

C **Who is talking? Choose the right name(s) for sentences 1–5.**
Wer spricht? Wählen Sie den/die richtigen Namen für die Sätze 1–5.

Mr Shrekly • Mrs Still • Tracy and Denzil • Lou • Tracy's parents

1 "Too bad you aren't coming this weekend, Lou." Mrs. Still
2 "Of course it's no problem that they're still living with us." Tracy's parents
3 "We aren't looking for a flat any more." Tracy and Denzil
4 "It's raining so I can't work in the garden anyway." Lou
5 "I can't understand why they're all running away …" Mrs Schrekly

D **Now you! Choose exercise 1 or 2.**
Wählen Sie Aufgabe 1 oder 2.

1 **Write an advert for your dream flat or house. (Tip: Look at page 32 for ideas.)**
Schreiben Sie eine Anzeige für Ihre Traumwohnung oder Ihr Traumhaus.

2 **Change Mrs Still's advert so that Tracy and Denzil will find her flat more interesting.**
Verändern Sie Mrs Stills Anzeige so, dass Tracy und Denzil ihre Wohnung interessanter finden.

Ziel: Ich kann in einem Geschäft als Kunde/Kundin oder Verkäufer/in ein Gespräch führen.

Getting started

A1.8 Sarah Brown from England has found a job in Germany. She is just moving into a place of her own. She wants to paint her flat, so she is going to a big shop.

Assistant	Kann ich Ihnen behilflich sein?
Sarah	Guten Abend. Ich ... Sorry, I don't speak German very well yet. Do you speak English?
Assistant	Yes, I do. How can I help you?
Sarah	I'm just moving into a new flat. I'm looking for paint and paintbrushes.
Assistant	They're over here. All the different colours and sizes. What colour are you looking for?
Sarah	Yellow.
Assistant	Here you are. Anything else?
Sarah	I'm trying to repair a window. Can I get wood here?
Assistant	Yes, of course. That way. My colleague over there will help you.
Sarah	Thank you for your help. Er, auf Wiedersehen.
Assistant	Thank you. Goodbye.

A Who says what? Choose exercise 1 or 2.

Wer sagt was? Wählen Sie Aufgabe 1 oder 2.

These statements and questions are from another dialogue between a customer and a shop assistant:

1. No, thanks. Bye. 8
2. Good morning. 1
3. Goodbye. 9
4. Hi. 2
5. Here you are. Anything else? 7
6. 3 How can I help you?
7. 4 I'm looking for nail polish.
8. 6 Black.
9. 5 Nail polish is over here. What colour are you looking for?

1 Find the 5 statements/questions that belong to the shop assistant.
Finden Sie die 5 Aussagen/Fragen, die zu dem/der Verkäufer/in gehören.
5, 6, 9, 2, 3

2 Write the complete dialogue in the right order.
Schreiben Sie das vollständige Gespräch in der richtigen Reihenfolge auf.

B Finish Sarah's email.

Vervollständigen Sie Sarahs Email.

Hi Robin

Thanks for your mail. **You're** busy? You can't be as busy as I am!

I'm sure you aren't painting [**1 not paint**] a new flat at the moment.

And you aren't repairing [**2 not repair**] windows right now.

Are you learning [**3 learn**] German too?

And are you starting [**4 start**] a new job?

See?! I must be the busiest girl in Germany. But it's all very exciting, and I love it!

Love
Sarah

to paint; paint malen, anstreichen; Farbe
(shop) assistant Verkäufer/in
paintbrush Farbpinsel
over here/there hier/dort
size Größe
Here you are. Hier, bitte.
Anything else? Noch etwas?
wood Holz
nail polish Nagellack

Ziel: Ich kann beim Einkaufen Dinge miteinander vergleichen.

In a flower shop

A1.9 Paula works in a flower shop. Today her customer is Vitali. He's looking for something unusual.

Paula Guten Tag. Sie wünschen?
Vitali Guten Tag. Eh, do you speak English?
Paula Well, I can try. What would you like?
Vitali I'm looking for a nice plant. I'm just moving into my new flat, you see. I'd like something unusual.
Paula OK. Here you are. This is the most unusual plant in the shop.
Vitali That looks fine, but it's too big. It should be smaller than that.
Paula Well, we've also got smaller plants. How about this one? But it isn't as unusual as the other one.
Vitali That's fine. How much does it cost?
Paula It isn't cheap. It's twelve euros.
Vitali That's more expensive than I thought.
Paula Well, it's the cheapest plant that we've got.
Vitali Well … OK, I'll take it. Thank you very much.

Grammar: Vergleiche → G11

smaller (than …) kleiner (als …)	**the cheapest** der/die/das billigste	**as unusual as …** so ungewöhnlich wie …
more expensive (than …) teurer (als …)	**the most unusual** der/die/das ungewöhnlichste	

Vocabulary: Wie etwas ist (Adjektive)

bad, beautiful, busy, cool, cold, dangerous, difficult, dirty, easy, great, famous, fantastic, fast, nasty, slow, terrible, unfriendly, warm

A **Look at the photos. Use the words in brackets and make sentences.**
Schauen Sie sich die Bilder an. Benutzen Sie die Wörter in den Klammern und bilden Sie Sätze.

1 [**small**] The brown dog ________ ________________________ than the black dog.
2 [**full**] The glass on the right ________ ________ ________________________ glass.
3 [**friendly**] The girl on the left looks as ________________________ as the girl on the right.

B **Match the beginnings (1–6) to the endings (A–F).**
EXAM Ordnen Sie die Satzanfänge (1–6) den Satzenden (A–F) zu.

C 1 Good morning. I'm looking for …
E 2 What would …
F 3 It's nice, but it's …
A 4 It should …
B 5 That's the cheapest interesting souvenir …
D 6 That's fine. How much …

A … be cheaper than that.
B … that we've got.
C … an interesting souvenir.
D … does it cost?
E … you like?
F … more expensive than I thought.

unusual
ungewöhnlich

What would you like?
Was wünschen Sie?

plant
Pflanze

I'd like …
Ich hätte gern …

Grammar Check 1: *Present progressive (I'm reading.)*

Kreuzen Sie die richtige Antwort an. Tragen Sie den Lösungsbuchstaben (nach dem Pfeil) unten auf der Seite ein.

1 Ich benutze das *present progressive*, um zu sagen, was ich

- A [ ] letztes Jahr gemacht habe. → D
- B [x] gerade mache. → T
- C [ ] immer wieder mache. → P

2 Ich bilde das *present progressive* mit *am/is/are* und einem Verb +

- A [ ] -s → M
- B [ ] -ed → R
- C [x] -ing → N

3 In einem Satz mit *present progressive* kann als Zeitangabe vorkommen:

- A [x] right now → R
- B [ ] yesterday → N
- C [ ] never → D

Grammar Check 2: Die *-ing*-Form

Kreuzen Sie das richtige Beispiel an. Tragen Sie den Lösungsbuchstaben (nach dem Pfeil) unten auf der Seite ein.

4 An die meisten Verben wird einfach *-ing* angehängt, z. B.

- A [ ] making → O
- B [x] cooking → R
- C [ ] cutting → G

5 Verben, die auf ein „stummes" *-e* enden, verlieren das *-e*, z. B.

- A [x] reading → A
- B [ ] putting → E
- C [x] writing → U

6 Endungen wie *-m*, *-n*, *-t* usw. werden manchmal verdoppelt, z. B.

- A [x] running → U
- B [ ] driving → E
- C [ ] walking → A

Grammar Check 3: Vergleiche

Kreuzen Sie die richtige Antwort an. Tragen Sie den Lösungsbuchstaben (nach dem Pfeil) unten auf der Seite ein.

7 Zwei unterschiedliche Dinge vergleiche ich mit

- A [ ] … then → E
- B [x] … than → I
- C [ ] … like → U

8 Die höchste Steigerung bei längeren Wörtern bilde ich mit

- A [ ] the must … → N
- B [ ] one most … → S
- C [x] the most … → E

9 Zwei gleiche Dinge vergleiche ich mit

- A [ ] as … than → V
- B [x] as … as → F
- C [ ] so … as → B

Tragen Sie die Lösungsbuchstaben hier ein. Sind alle Fragen richtig beantwortet, ergibt sich ein Wort aus dieser Unit.

9	6	4	2	7	1	5	3	8
F	U	R	N	I	T	U	R	E

Vocabulary Check 1: Das richtige Wort

Kreuzen Sie jeweils die **drei** richtigen Antworten an. Tragen Sie die Lösungsbuchstaben (nach dem Pfeil) der Reihe nach unten ein.

1 Zimmer in einer Wohnung oder einem Haus:

- A [x] bathroom → P
- B [ ] flat → E
- C [x] kitchen → A
- D [x] bedroom → I
- E [ ] apartment → L

2 Tätigkeiten, die man in der Küche ausführt:

- A [x] cut → N
- B [x] cook → T
- C [x] wash → B
- D [ ] sleep → D
- E [ ] swim → E

3 Beschreibungen:

- A [ ] repair → L
- B [x] big → R
- C [x] yellow → U
- D [ ] sizes → C
- E [x] terrible → S

4 Menschen:

- A [ ] colour → T
- B [x] shop assistant → H
- C [x] customer → E
- D [ ] smaller → R
- E [x] tourist → S

Lösungswort (Mehrzahl):

P	A	I	N	T	B	R	U	S	H	E	S
Frage 1			Frage 2			Frage 3			Frage 4		

Vocabulary Check 2: Gegensätze

Wählen Sie das richtige Wort aus der Reihe, um Gegensätze zu den Wörtern 1–6 zu bilden. Tragen Sie dann den Lösungsbuchstaben weiter unten ein.

bad R • expensive C • fantastic N • full A • modern T • nice O • old R • tall E • terrible I

1 good – bad

2 cheap – expensive

3 traditional – modern

4 new – old

5 empty – full

6 unfriendly – nice

Lösungswort:

2	5	4	1	6	3
C	A	R	R	O	T

Video lounge

V3 BBC Motion Gallery

The Grand Canyon Skywalk

A **Before you watch the video: Think about the question and answer it.**
Bevor Sie sich das Video ansehen: Denken Sie über die Frage nach und beantworten Sie sie.

Ist der Grand Canyon

- A [ ] ein Naturwunder?
- B [ ] ein Kulturdenkmal?

B **After watching the video: True or false?**
Nach dem Ansehen des Videos: Richtig oder falsch?

1 Tourists can look down at the canyon from a walkway.

A [ ] true B [ ] false

2 1200 people can use the walkway at the same time.

A [ ] true B [ ] false

Different shops

A Jobs in a department store

1 Look at the phrases and underline the verbs.

- cut fabric for customers
- get things for customers
- put things on shelves
- help customers
- keep the shop clean
- make contact with the customers
- take money from customers
- unpack things
- sell things
- wrap things for customers
- use a computer
- write answers to emails

2 Put the verbs in the -ing form and write them in the table below.

unverändert	ohne -e	verdoppelter Buchstabe
		cutting

B In the department store: What are they doing?

Complete the sentences with the present progressive. Use the verbs in brackets.

1 Where's Ahmed? __________ he __________ [**write**] an email?
– No, he isn't. He __________ [**talk**] to a customer.

2 Where's Rosie? __________ she __________ [**have**] lunch?
– No, she isn't. She __________ [**help**] Ms Lowe.

3 Where are Paul and Dinah? __________ they __________ [**clean**] the windows?
– No, they aren't. They __________ [**put**] new shirts on the shelves.

4 And you? What __________ you __________ [**do**] at the moment?
– Well, I __________ [**answer**] your questions!

Grammar: ***Simple present*** **oder** ***present progressive*****?** → G1+2

– *simple present*: wenn etwas regelmäßig geschieht
– *present progressive*: wenn etwas gerade jetzt geschieht

department store
Kaufhaus

fabric
Stoff

to make contact
Kontakt herstellen, ansprechen

to unpack
auspacken

to wrap
einwickeln

C In a tattoo shop

Choose the simple present or the present progressive to complete the sentences. Circle the right form.

1. My sister Becca | works | is working | in a tattoo shop on Saturdays.
2. It's a busy shop. She often | stays | is staying | till late.
3. "Becca, quick, the phone | rings | is ringing | !"
4. Becca says that a lot of people | choose | are choosing | a fake tattoo.
5. "Becca, | do you watch | are you watching | the teenagers over there?"
6. Becca is at home now. | She counts | She's counting | her money!

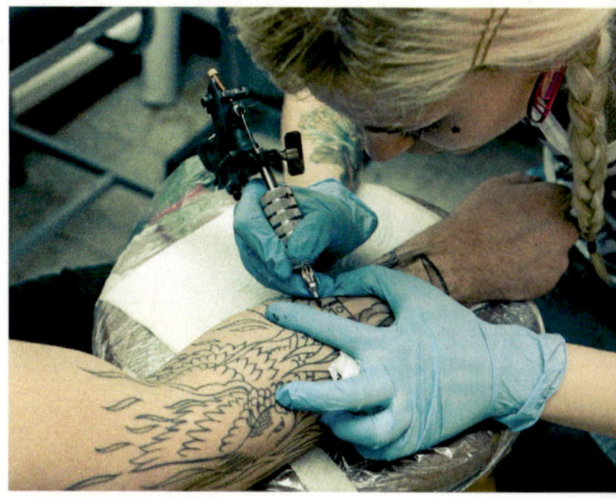

D In a furniture shop

Think carefully: Which is the right answer, A or B?

1. The shop assistant is just answering
   - A [x] two customers' questions.
   - B [ ] two customer's questions.
2.
   - A [x] Bills' mother
   - B [x] Bill's mother

   is just paying for his new table.
3. The man over there doesn't like
   - A [x] the colour of the cupboard.
   - B [ ] the colour from the cupboard.
4.
   - A [x] Mrs Miller's kid
   - B [ ] The kid's Mrs Miller

   is just trying out the sofa.

E In a souvenir shop

Compare the souvenirs. Complete the sentences. Use the **blue** adjective.

Tip: – *than* im Satz = erste Steigerung
– *the* oder *the most* vor der Lücke = höchste Steigerung

1. The flag is **nice**, but I think the T-shirt is nicer than the flag.
2. The pencil is **cool**, but I think the little bear is the coolest souvenir in the shop.
3. This toy is **terrible**, but I'm sure that toy is the most terrible toy in the world!
4. The cup is **expensive**, but the mug is more expensive than the cup.

F Mike's plans

Put the words/phrases in the right order and make sentences.

1. | own. | place | Mike is | for a | looking | of his |
   Mike is looking for a place of his own
2. | his parents' | at the moment. | house | living in | He's |
   He's living in his parents' house at the moment
3. | furniture | buying new | flat. | for his | Mike is |
   Mike is buying new furniture for his flat.
4. | in | putting it | garage. | He's | his parents' |
   He's putting it in his parents' garage.
5. | the | country! | garage | It's | in the | fullest |
   It's the fullest garage in the country

to count
zählen

Textarbeit: Mediation

A1.23

The great English breakfast

It is true that a good English breakfast never lets you down. There is no better way to start a new day than with fried eggs and bacon, a sausage or two, tomatoes, and, if you like, even mushrooms. Toast and marmalade follow and you have it with a pot of tea.

Of course, people often only have toast and marmalade for breakfast on weekdays because they do not have the time for a full breakfast. A fry-up (another name for a cooked breakfast) is often only eaten on Saturday or Sunday mornings.

Today cafés and supermarkets also serve a fry-up at lunchtime. Moreover, there are many traditional cafés in Britain that serve breakfast throughout the day. The full breakfast may therefore be on the menu as the "all day breakfast". Such cafés are typically used by builders or lorry drivers. That is why the very strong tea that is served in such cafés is known as "builder's tea". (163 words)

Annotations:
line 2 **to let someone down** – jemanden im Stich lassen
line 3 **fried** – gebraten
line 5 **mushrooms** – Pilze
line 15 **moreover** – darüber hinaus
line 20 **builder** – Bauarbeiter

Skills Tip: ***Mediation*** **ist eine Verständnisübung. Sie schreiben auf Deutsch.**

- Lesen Sie zuerst, **wo bzw. für wen** Sie den Text wiedergeben sollen. Das bestimmt den Ton Ihres Textes.
- Lesen Sie dann die **Punkte** und schreiben Sie ganze Sätze zu jedem Punkt. Ziel ist ein zusammenhängender deutscher Text.
- **Wichtig:** Übersetzen Sie den Text nicht Wort für Wort, sondern geben Sie den Inhalt des Textes sinngemäß wieder.

Sie haben Sprachferien in England verbracht und berichten **in Ihrer Schülerzeitung** vom „typischen“ englischen Frühstück.
Geben Sie den Text **sinngemäß auf Deutsch** wieder.
Schreiben Sie bitte einen **zusammenhängenden Text**.
Informieren Sie Ihre Mitschüler über folgende **Punkte**:

- erster Gang eines typischen englischen Frühstücks
- zusätzliche Bestandteile eines englischen Frühstücks
- Frühstück in England an normalen Wochentagen
- Zeitpunkt für ein typisches englisches Frühstück
- Frühstück außer Haus
- „Bauarbeiter-Tee“

Managing Situations: Talking to people – Telephoning

Skills Tip: ***Telephoning*** **ist eine Zuordnungsübung.**

- Lesen Sie gründlich die **Situationsbeschreibung** über dem Dialog und alle Aussagen.
- Suchen Sie **Begrüßung** und Verabschiedung und ordnen Sie sie am Anfang bzw. am Ende des Gesprächs ein.
- Achten Sie auf **Wortwiederholungen** in Frage und Antwort.
- Stellen Sie fest, welche Fragen mit **Yes/No** beantwortet werden können und suchen Sie nach solchen Satzanfängen.
- Achten Sie auf **Fragewörter**, die gezielt nach etwas fragen (*How many? How much? When?* usw.) und suchen Sie nach der passenden Antwort.
- Prüfen Sie nach der Zuordnung, ob auch die nächste Reaktion des Gesprächspartners passt.

Colin Davis works for a supermarket. He takes orders from customers.
Here is one of his telephone conversations. Find the phrases A–H of a caller that fit into 1–8.

Colin: Brendon Superstores, Colin Davis speaking.
1 Caller: E
Colin: Hi Margaret, how are you?
2 Caller: G
Colin: What can I do for you, Margaret?
3 Caller: F
Colin: I see. So it's tea, milk, butter, eggs, white bread and ham, **right**?
4 Caller: H
Colin: **How many** would you like to have?
5 Caller: A
Colin: You will love them! They really taste wonderful.
6 Caller: C
Colin: What time do you want delivery tomorrow?
7 Caller: B
Colin: Yes, no problem. **Are you coming** to the social club tonight?
8 Caller: D
Colin: See you then, Margaret. Bye-bye.

A I'll have **two** with chocolate and **five** cupcakes.
B Is ten o'clock OK?
C I know. I tried them when I was at a friend's house. They are lovely.
D **Yes**, of course. I don't want to miss it.
E **Hello Colin. This is Margaret Woods.**
F Well, it's just my weekly order, Colin.
G Thanks, I'm fine.
H **Yes, that's right.** Hold on – Rosie is coming to see me tomorrow. So I'll need some cakes.

4 On the move

Ziel: Ich kann sagen, was in der Vergangenheit geschah. *Beispiel: Yesterday I watched TV. (simple past)*

A What did these people do last summer? First look at the photos.
Was haben diese Menschen letzten Sommer gemacht? Sehen Sie sich zuerst die Fotos an.

1

Liv, Mark, Anna and Pedro

2

Hassan

3

Marisa

Who said what? Read the statements and tick the right number.
Wer sagte was? Lesen Sie die Aussagen und machen Sie ein Häkchen an die passende Zahl.

☐ 1 ☐ 2 ☐ 3 In the last summer holidays I took driving lessons.

☐ 1 ☐ 2 ☐ 3 Last August we all flew to Spain and rented a car there.

☐ 1 ☐ 2 ☐ 3 Last summer I bought an old car and repaired it.

Vocabulary: Fortbewegung

- to cycle, to drive, to fly, to ride, to walk
- bike, bus, camper van, car, jeep, lorry, motorbike, plane, train, truck, van

Grammar: Was in der Vergangenheit geschah → G 3

- regelmäßig: Verb + -ed
- unregelmäßig: besondere Formen
  → vordere Umschlagseite (innen)

Last week I walked to town.
Letzte Woche ging ich zu Fuß in die Stadt.

Pat drove to London yesterday.
Pat fuhr gestern nach London.

B What about people who you know?
Was ist mit den Menschen, die Sie kennen?

Last summer ______________________ stayed at home in the holidays.

Last year ______________________ took driving lessons.

____

on the move
in Bewegung

driving lessons
Fahrstunden

we flew
wir flogen (Grundform: to fly)

Spain
Spanien

to rent
mieten

to cycle
Rad fahren

camper van
Wohnmobil

lorry, truck
LKW

van
(Klein-)Transporter

Rent-a-Wreck

A **Listen to Sue's story. Tick the right picture (1–3).**
A1.10 Hören Sie sich Sues Geschichte an. Machen Sie ein Häkchen an das passende Bild (1–3).

1  ☐
2  ☐
3  ☐

B **Listen to the story again. Tick *true* or *false* for sentences 1–4.**
Hören Sie sich die Geschichte noch einmal an. Machen Sie bei den Sätzen 1–4 ein Häkchen bei *richtig* oder *falsch*.

		true	false
1	Sue's brother Tim couldn't pick her up because he was too busy.	☐	☐
2	Sue wanted to rent a camper van but it was too expensive.	☐	☐
3	Sue went to Denver by bus and bought an old car.	☐	☐
4	Tim had an accident in a modern camper van.	☐	☐

Grammar: Vergangenheit – regelmäßige Verben → G 3

Verb	+	-ed
walk	→	walked
cycle	→	cycled
try	→	tried
stop	→	stopped

C **Summer holidays. Fill in the correct word.**
EXAM Sommerferien. Fügen Sie das richtige Wort ein.

Example: → *Yesterday we made [**thought/made**] plans for the summer holidays.*

1 Last year we ______________ [went/wrote] on a hiking trip to the south of Germany.

2 But the weather last summer was awful – it ______________ [rained/ran] all the time!

3 So yesterday I ______________ [liked/looked] at flights on the internet.

4 My friend Alina ______________ [said/told] me about a good website last week.

5 She ______________ [booked/rented] her flights there last year.

6 Last August she ______________ [flew/knew] to Spain for two weeks.

wreck
Wrack

to pick somebody up
jemanden abholen

accident
Unfall

hiking trip
Wandertour

flight
Flug

My first car

A1.11 Sharon had her driving test last week. Did she pass it? What do you think? Find out if you were right.

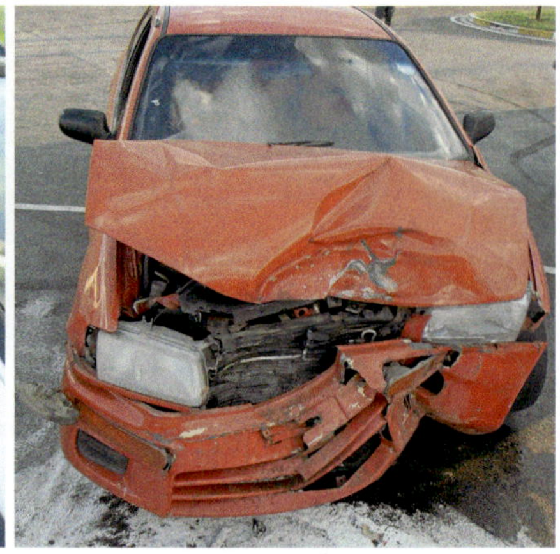

Yesterday Sharon talked to her uncle Bob.

Uncle Bob: Hello, Sharon. So you passed your driving test first time? Well done!

Sharon: Thanks, Uncle Bob. It was a lot easier than I thought. Now the next problem is buying a car.

Uncle Bob: Ah, yes. I remember my first car. It was a used car of course, but quite modern for the time. It had a CD player instead of a cassette player! We all thought that cassette players were – what do you young people say – "they were *so* old technology"! Of course there weren't any MP3 players or satnavs yet. But I didn't need a satnav – I just used a map.

Sharon: Oh, I see.

Uncle Bob: But let me tell you about my first trip in my new car. I was a little nervous. I wanted to go to a party. My boot was full of drinks because I was the only person who had a car. I really didn't want to have an accident! But I wanted to listen to my new CD. So I looked away from the road for two seconds while I opened the CD case and put the CD into the player. Suddenly I was on the wrong side of the road and crashed my car into a phone box! After that my car was a wreck. The boys at the party were very unhappy – their drinks never came! And your grandad was very angry. He bought me the car, you see.

Sharon: Wow. Did grandad buy you another car?

Uncle Bob: Of course not. I had to ride my bike again! Now tell me, you're going to see your boyfriend in Wickham now, aren't you? That's about ten minutes from here by car.

Sharon: Yeah, but it's half an hour by bus!

Uncle Bob: Forget the bus, Sharon. You can drive my old car – with your new driving licence. It's in my garage.

Sharon: Really? Well, thank you, Uncle Bob!

Uncle Bob: That's OK. Just put the CD in *before* you start, OK?

Sharon: CD? That's *so* old technology!

used – gebraucht
quite – ziemlich
instead of – statt
cassette – Kassette
technology – Technologie
satnav – Satelliten-navigationssystem, „Navi"
boot – Kofferraum
case – Behälter
to crash the car into something – mit dem Auto in etwas hineinkrachen
phone box – Telefonzelle
after that – danach
driving licence – Führerschein

Vocabulary: Auto fahren

- to take driving lessons, to pass a driving test, to have a driving licence
- to drive a car, to ride a (motor)bike, to go by bus, to take a train
- to crash a car into something, to have an accident

A EXAM **Decide if these statements are true or false. Write your answer after the statement.**
Entscheiden Sie, ob diese Aussagen richtig oder falsch sind. Schreiben Sie Ihre Antwort hinter die Aussage.

Skills Tip

Lesen Sie sich die Aussage in Ruhe durch. Vergleichen Sie sie mit der passenden Stelle im Text, bevor Sie entscheiden.

	Statement	true or false?
1	Sharon thinks the driving test was difficult.	false
2	Uncle Bob's first car had a satnav.	
3	Uncle Bob had an accident when he used the CD player.	
4	Uncle Bob's father bought him another car.	
5	It takes 30 minutes to get to Wickham by bus.	

B EXAM **Find the right word in the text for definitions 1–5.**
Finden Sie zu den Worterklärungen 1–5 das passende Wort im Text.

1. A plan that shows roads, towns, rivers, etc.: map
2. A place in a car that you use for bags, etc.: ______
3. A box for CDs: ______
4. The man who is the father of your father or mother: ______
5. A building for one or more cars: ______

Grammar: Beschreibungen → G10

Sachen: **I bought the car which/that we looked at last week.**
Ich habe das Auto, das wir uns letzte Woche ansahen, gekauft.

Personen: **The woman who/that drives the blue car is my boss.**
Die Frau, die das blaue Auto fährt, ist meine Chefin.

C **Circle the right time phrase.**
Umkringeln Sie die richtige Zeitangabe.

Example: → *My colleague flew to Spain* *last month* (circled) | *right now*.

1. I parked my car behind the garage | usually | yesterday |.
2. Did Marija take her driving test | last week | tomorrow |?
3. I can't talk | now | last summer |, I'm driving!
4. The man who is running after the ball | at this moment | last night | is my friend Jack.

Grammar: do/does (simple present) → did (simple past) → G1+3

Does Bob often watch TV?	→ **Did Bob watch TV last night?**
Sieht Bob oft fern?	Hat Bob gestern Abend ferngesehen?

Ziel: Ich kann Reisewege beschreiben.

How do I get to . . .?

A1.12 Jan is from Holland. He started work as an employee at a building firm only three weeks ago. Now he's talking to Karen.

Jan So how do I get to Westwood tomorrow?
Karen Well, do you want to go by car or use public transport?
Jan I'm not sure. I don't have to go by car. My appointment is at 9.30 a.m.
Karen You shouldn't go by car then. The traffic is terrible at that time. The best thing is to take the 8.45 train to Eastwood Station. Be careful: You mustn't take the 8.48 – it's a fast train that doesn't stop at Eastwood.
Jan OK. Do I have to change trains?
Karen No, that's not necessary. The train goes right through to Eastwood. When you get off the train, you should look for a taxi. The bus service to Westwood is awful.
Jan OK, Karen. Thanks for your help.

Vocabulary: sollen – müssen – nicht dürfen

You **should take** the bus.
Du solltest den Bus nehmen.
I have to be home at 8 o'clock.
Ich muss um 8 Uhr zu Hause sein.
He mustn't turn right.
Er darf (!) nicht rechts abbiegen.

A **Match the English sentences 1–3 to the German sentences A-C. Draw lines.**
Ordnen Sie die englischen Sätze 1–3 den deutschen Sätzen A-C zu. Ziehen Sie Linien.

1 You should turn left there.	A Du darfst dort nicht links abbiegen.
2 You don't have to turn left there.	B Du solltest dort links abbiegen.
3 You mustn't turn left there.	C Du musst dort nicht links abbiegen.

B **Two days later . . . Choose exercise 1 or 2.**
Zwei Tage später . . . Wählen Sie Aufgabe 1 oder 2.

1 **Jan did everything wrong. Put in the missing verbs.**
Jan hat alles falsch gemacht. Fügen Sie die fehlenden Verben ein.

arrived • got • paid • took • used • was

Karen Hi Jan. How ____________ [1] your trip to Westwood yesterday?
Jan Well, I followed your advice and ____________ [2] public transport. Unfortunately, I ____________ [3] the wrong train. It was the 8.48 and it went right through to Bristol Station. So I ____________ [4] off there and took a taxi back to Westwood. I ____________ [5] in time for my appointment – but I ____________ [6] a lot of money!

2 **Jan did everything right. Use the help below and write his story.**
Jan hat alles richtig gemacht. Benutzen Sie die Hilfe unten und schreiben Sie seine Geschichte.

"It was great, thanks again. I followed your advice and . . . public transport. I . . . the right . . . It was the . . . to . . . I . . . there and . . . taxi. I didn't . . . the bus to Westwood – and I . . . in time for my appointment."

to get (to . . .) (nach . . .) kommen, gelangen
employee Angestellte/r
building firm Baufirma
three weeks ago vor drei Wochen
public transport öffentlicher Nahverkehr
mustn't nicht dürfen
to change trains umsteigen
necessary nötig
right through direkt durch
to get off aussteigen
you should du solltest
to turn left/right links/rechts abbiegen
to follow folgen, befolgen
advice Ratschlag
in time rechtzeitig, pünktlich

Ziel: Ich kann Wegbeschreibungen geben.

Giving directions

A1.13

Last month Mia and Finn were on holiday in Newtown. They wanted to go to the department store. But they were lost. So they asked a young man: "Excuse me, could you tell us the way to the department store, please?"

"Yes, of course," he said. "Go straight ahead. Cross High Street. The department store is behind the hospital on the left."

"No, it's not!" said a woman who stood next to them. "You're sending them to the tourist information! Listen. First you have to cross the road. Then you should go straight ahead and turn right into High Street over there. Go along High Street. Cross King Street. The department store is on your right, opposite the church."

This heard a policeman who came past. "Opposite the church? That's the pub! Now listen to me. Go straight ahead. Follow Green Street until you get to Market Street and turn right there. The department store is on the other side of Market Street, next to the post office."

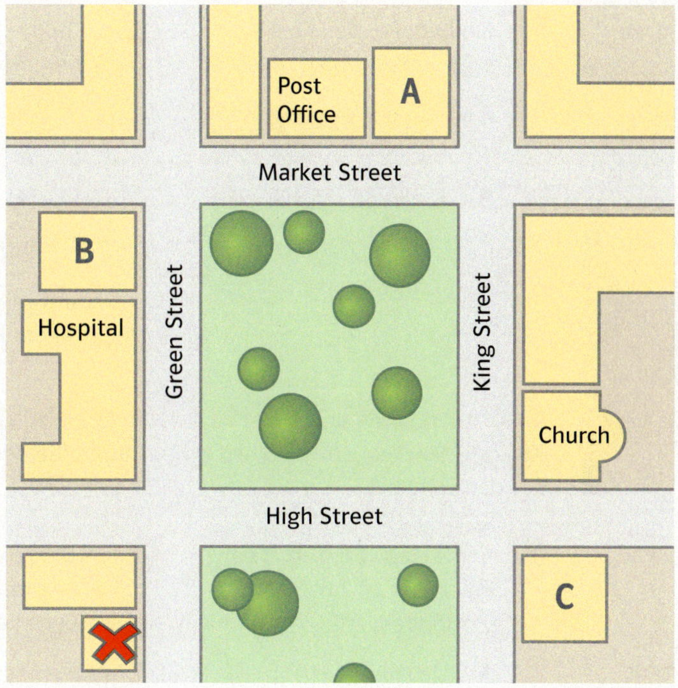

A **Look at the map. Mia and Finn are at X. Now read the text carefully. What buildings are A, B and C?**
Sehen Sie sich die Karte an. Mia und Finn befinden sich bei X. Lesen Sie nun aufmerksam den Text. Was sind A, B und C für Gebäude?

A: ____________ B: ____________ C: ____________

B **Look at the map. Read the directions and circle the right words.**
Sehen Sie sich die Karte an. Lesen Sie die Wegbeschreibungen und umkringeln Sie die richtigen Wörter.

1. How do I get from the church to the post office? – Turn right into King Street. Go along King Street. Then turn [left] [right] into [Green] [Market] Street. It's [behind] [opposite] the department store.
2. How do I get from the hospital to the church? – Go straight ahead until you get to High Street. Turn left. Go along [High] [Market] Street. Then [cross] [go along] King Street. It's [behind] [opposite] the pub.

Vocabulary: **Wo? Wohin?**
- at, behind, between, in, in front of, next to, on, opposite, under
- across, along, down, from, into, off, over, through, to

Vocabulary: **Wegbeschreibung**
- cross/follow/go along High Street
- go straight ahead, turn left/right

directions
Wegbeschreibung

department store
Kaufhaus

to be lost
sich verlaufen/verirrt haben

straight ahead
geradeaus

to cross
überqueren

next to
neben

along
entlang

opposite
gegenüber (von)

church
Kirche

pub
Kneipe

between
zwischen

in front of
vor

Grammar Check 1: *Simple past (I watched TV.)*

Kreuzen Sie die richtige Antwort an. Tragen Sie den Lösungsbuchstaben (nach dem Pfeil) unten auf der Seite ein.

1 Ich benutze das *simple past*, um zu sagen, was ich

A ☐ in der Vergangenheit gemacht habe. → N

B ☐ gerade mache. → T

C ☐ in der Zukunft machen werde. → S

2 Ich bilde das *simple past* mit einem regelmäßigen Verb und

A ☐ -s → A

B ☐ -ed → O

C ☐ -ing → R

oder mit einem unregelmäßigen Verb.

3 Für Fragen und Verneinungen im *simple past* brauche ich

A ☐ did → E

B ☐ done → I

C ☐ do/does → A

Grammar Check 2: *Simple past* – regelmäßige Verben

Kreuzen Sie das richtige Beispiel an. Tragen Sie den Lösungsbuchstaben (nach dem Pfeil) unten auf der Seite ein.

4 Endungen wie *-l*, *-n*, *-t* usw. werden manchmal verdoppelt, z. B.

A ☐ walked → L

B ☐ used → R

C ☐ travelled → P

5 Verben, die auf ein „stummes" *-e* enden, verlieren das *-e*, z. B.

A ☐ need → B

B ☐ watched → G

C ☐ arrived → T

6 Aus einem *-y* am Ende wird oft ein *-i* + *-ed*, z. B.

A ☐ repaired → L

B ☐ tried → P

C ☐ stayed → C

Grammar Check 3: Beschreibungen

Kreuzen Sie die richtige Antwort an. Tragen Sie den Lösungsbuchstaben (nach dem Pfeil) unten auf der Seite ein.

7 Wenn ich Sachen näher beschreiben will, kann ich

A ☐ which → I

B ☐ when → U

C ☐ how → R

benutzen.

8 Wenn ich Personen näher beschreiben will, kann ich

A ☐ what → S

B ☐ where → T

C ☐ who → N

benutzen.

9 Wenn ich Sachen <u>oder</u> Personen näher beschreiben will, kann ich

A ☐ the → O

B ☐ that → A

C ☐ than → E

benutzen.

Tragen Sie die Lösungsbuchstaben hier ein. Sind alle Fragen richtig beantwortet, ergibt sich ein Wort aus dieser Unit.

9	6	4	2	7	8	5		3	1	
							M			T

Vocabulary Check 1: Ein Wort passt nicht

Kreuzen Sie das Wort an, das **nicht** in den Satz passt. Tragen Sie den Lösungsbuchstaben (nach dem Pfeil) weiter unten ein.

1 Yesterday I
- A ☐ drove → P
- B ☐ walked → E
- C ☐ slept → I
- D ☐ cycled → R

to work.

2 I work as a driver. I drive a
- A ☐ lorry. → N
- B ☐ bike. → H
- C ☐ truck. → E
- D ☐ bus. → D

3 The hospital is next to the
- A ☐ pub. → R
- B ☐ employee. → L
- C ☐ church. → U
- D ☐ department store. → A

4 The shop is
- A ☐ behind → D
- B ☐ in front of → S
- C ☐ opposite → E
- D ☐ quite → T

the station.

5 I've just bought a
- A ☐ furnished → G
- B ☐ modern → E
- C ☐ used → C
- D ☐ fast → A

car.

6 The church? Just
- A ☐ go along → G
- B ☐ turn left into → B
- C ☐ move out of → F
- D ☐ cross → A

High Street.

Lösungswort:

6 ☐ 3 ☐ 1 ☐ 5 ☐ 2 ☐ 4 ☐

Vocabulary Check 2: Partnerwörter

Finden Sie für die Wörter 1–6 das richtige Partnerwort. Ziehen Sie Linien. Tragen Sie dann den Lösungsbuchstaben unten ein.

1 hiking	van → D
2 camper	transport → V
3 driving	trip → C
4 phone	licence → I
5 public	store → A
6 department	box → E

Lösungswort:

6 ☐ 2 ☐ 5 ☐ 3 ☐ 1 ☐ 4 ☐

Video lounge

V4 BBC Motion Gallery

Out and about in New York City

What does the video NOT talk about? Tick one word in each group.
Was wird im Video NICHT erwähnt? Machen Sie ein Häkchen an ein Wort in jeder Gruppe.

1
- A ☐ taxis
- B ☐ buses
- C ☐ subway trains

2
- A ☐ maps
- B ☐ directions
- C ☐ satnavs

3
- A ☐ water towers
- B ☐ banks
- C ☐ skyscrapers

4
- A ☐ cakes
- B ☐ sandwiches
- C ☐ hot dogs

A Crossword

Put in the simple past forms of the irregular verbs.

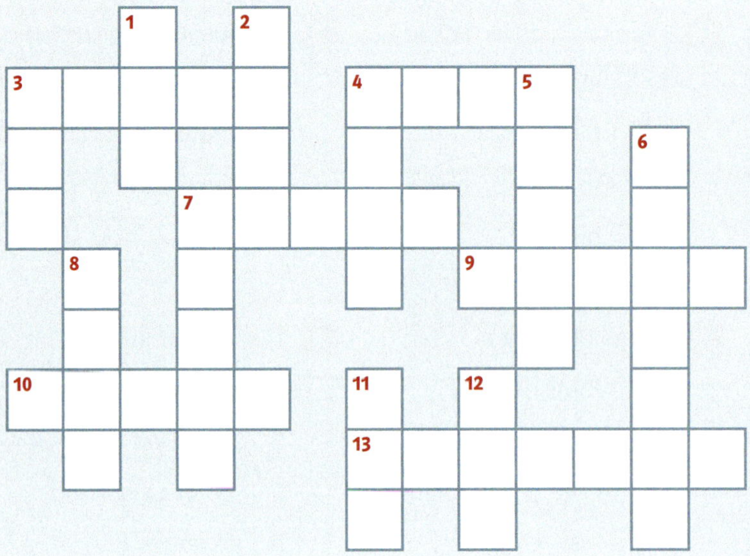

Waagerecht →
3 to drive
4 to know
7 to sleep
9 to stand
10 to break
13 to think

Senkrecht ↓
1 to get
2 to fall
3 to do
4 to keep
5 to write
6 to bring
7 to speak
8 to wear
11 to eat
12 to win

B The Liverpool flat

Complete the sentences with the simple past form of the verbs in brackets.

1 Khalid ______________ **[work]** in Liverpool last month.

2 He ______________ **[not need]** a hotel room because his firm has a place for their workers there.

3 He ______________ **[enter]** the address in his satnav.

4 He ______________ **[not expect]** a special place.

5 But when he ______________ **[get]** there, he was surprised.

6 The flat there was so big and nice, he almost ______________ **[not want]** to go home again.

C On the move

Complete the sentences with the verbs in brackets. You have to use the simple present and the simple past each time.

Example: → *[go] We usually go on holiday in August. But last year we went in July.*

1 **[ride]** Alice often ______________ her bike.
Last week she ______________ about 200 kilometres on it.

2 **[drive]** Joe ______________ his truck to Dresden yesterday.
He normally ______________ to Berlin.

3 **[fly]** We always ______________ to Spain.
But a year ago we ______________ to Turkey.

4 **[walk]** Yesterday I ______________ to town.
I don't often ______________.

5 **[take]** Last month it ______________ me 90 minutes to get to the airport.
Sometimes it only ______________ 60 minutes.

to expect erwarten
surprised überrascht
normally normalerweise
a year ago vor einem Jahr
Turkey die Türkei

D Truck driver Carl
Circle the right word.

1. Last week I listened to the advice | that | the | my colleague Carl gave me.
2. Carl is one of the young men | how | who | drive a truck for our company.
3. So last week I took the road to York | what | which | Carl recommended.
4. But it took longer than the road | that | who | I normally take.
5. The customer | what | who | wanted to see me wasn't very happy.
6. When I told Carl about this later, he laughed. "Oh, sorry – truck drivers | which | who | want a good breakfast always take that road. It takes longer, but we all love Jill's breakfast cafe there."

E Giving directions
Pick the right word and complete the sentences. You don't need all the words.

after the • ahead • along • between • cross • front • left • next • off • opposite • turn • under the

"Excuse me, how can I get to …

1. … Cora's Cafe?" – "Go ______ Park Street. Turn ______ into Elm Street. Cora's Cafe is ______ to the museum."
2. … the park?" – "______ the street and ______ left into Maple Street. The park is right in ______ of you."
3. … the cinema?" – "Go straight ______. Turn right into Baker Street ______ department store. The cinema is on your left, ______ the pub."

F Mo's lunch cafe
Put the phrases in the right order and make sentences.

1. | favourite lunch cafe | last week I | near York | stopped at my |

______.

2. | because Mo | I always | is my sister | stop there | is great | and her lunch |

______.

3. | and got up | very busy, so | my lunch | the cafe was | I quickly ate |

______.

4. | the door, two | when I | grabbed my arms | got to | police officers suddenly |

______.

5. | believe me | that I never | have to pay at Mo's | when I said | they didn't |

______.

6. | she came | to Mo and | I shouted | and explained | the situation |

______.

to recommend empfehlen

to grab packen, grapschen

to believe glauben

Textarbeit: Statement

A1.24

Crossing Australia

Not long ago, the "Ghan" made its first trip from Adelaide to Darwin. So today passengers can cross Australia from coast to coast by train.

It all started in 1929 when the first Ghan train line was opened and ran from Adelaide in the south to Alice Springs, which is in the middle of Australia – just a few hours from Ayers Rock. Before that, Afghan immigrants had used camels in the dry deserts there. So the first train was called the "Ghan" – short for the "Afghan". You can still see a picture of a camel on the front of the locomotives.

Today it takes two days to travel the 3,000 km through the fifth continent because the train only has a top speed of about 115 km per hour. Of course, it is much faster and also cheaper to go by plane. But passengers who take the train do this because they want to enjoy the beautiful scenery. There are some two-hour stops on the way so that they can visit interesting places or even take a ride on a camel. (183 words)

Annotations:
title **to cross** – durchqueren
line 9 **Afghan immigrants** – afghanische Einwanderer
line 10 **desert** – Wüste

Skills Tip: In *Statement* geht es um Ihre Meinung.

- Lesen Sie zuerst die **Aussage** gründlich.
- Zu dieser Aussage müssen Sie nun in einem kurzen Text Stellung nehmen.
- Die Fragen ***„Why? Why not?"*** (Warum? Warum nicht?) bedeuten, dass Sie Ihre Meinung begründen müssen.
- **Idee:** Sammeln Sie zuerst alle Argumente **dafür (+)** und **dagegen (–)** (also für die Aussage und gegen die Aussage). Schreiben Sie die Argumente in **Stichpunkten** auf (siehe nächste Seite).
- Bilden Sie sich eine Meinung.
- Formulieren Sie die Stichpunkte in **ganzen englischen Sätzen**.
- Ihre eigene Meinung können Sie mit *„I think …"* oder *„I believe …"* einleiten.
- Sie sollen 40 – 50 Wörter schreiben. Wie viel ist das? Dies sind 40 „Wörter":
  Xxxxx xx xxxxx xxx xxxx xx xxxxx xxx xxxx xx xxxxxxx xxx xxxxx xxxxxxxxx xxxxxxx xxx xxxxx xxxx xxx x xxx xxxxx xx xxxxx xx xxx xxxx. Xx xxxxxx, xx xx xxxx xxxxx xxx xxxx xxxxxxx xx xx xx xxxxx.

Some people say, "Travelling by train is better than travelling by plane."
Do you think they are right? **Why? Why not?** Give your opinion.
Write 40 – 50 words in complete English sentences, please.

Beispiele für Stichpunkte:
+ enjoy beautiful scenery / visit interesting places on the way / meet other people
– takes a long time / very expensive / boring at night

Managing Situations: Giving directions

Skills Tip: Wiederholen Sie die Redemittel zur Wegbeschreibung (S. 47).

- Sie sollen hier eine Wegbeschreibung auf Englisch abgeben.
- Sehen Sie sich den Auszug aus dem Stadtplan gut an und finden Sie Ihren **Standort**.
- Lesen Sie die Aufgabe. Finden Sie den **gesuchten Ort** auf der Karte.
- Zeichnen Sie sich jetzt den Weg von Ihrem **Standort** zum **gesuchten Ort** in den Stadtplan ein.
- Geben Sie dann die Wegbeschreibung in mehreren ganzen Sätzen ab. Verwenden Sie die Redemittel zur Wegbeschreibung.

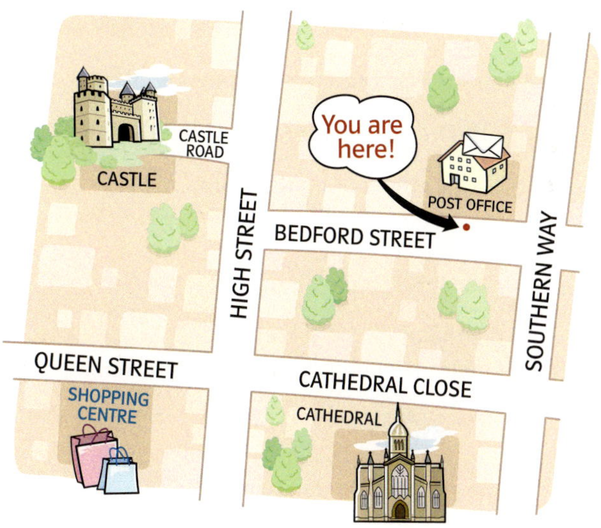

You are standing in front of the post office in Bedford Street.
A girl asks you: "Can you tell me the way to the **shopping centre**, please?"
Tell her how to get there.

s6wi47

5 You need me!

Ziel: Ich kann sagen, was ich in der Zukunft tun werde. *Beispiel: I'll work. (future)*

A What will Ben and Elena do? Read the dialogue.
Was werden Ben und Elena tun? Lesen Sie den Dialog.

1. Ben, what will you do after school next year?

I'm good at repairing things. So I hope that I'll find a job as a car mechanic.

2. Really? But the firms won't take you without an apprenticeship.

That's OK. What about your plans for the future, Elena?

3. I won't start a family soon. First I'll do an apprenticeship as a hairdresser. Later I'll have my own salon.

Sounds great. I'm sure there'll be lots of opportunities for us.

What are Ben and Elena talking about?

1 their past, their present or their future – ______

2 jobs, school or relationships – ______

Vocabulary: Fähigkeiten

I'm good at …
languages, listening, maths, organizing, talking, using a computer, working with my hands, writing

Grammar: Was in der Zukunft (nicht) geschehen wird → G 5

will (Kurzform 'll) + Verb	will not (Kurzform won't) + Verb
I'll start an apprenticeship next year. Nächstes Jahr werde ich eine Ausbildung anfangen.	**In the future Sharif won't work at Webb's any more.** In der Zukunft wird Sharif nicht mehr für Webb's arbeiten.

B What about you?
Und Sie?

In ten years I'll ______

______

______

car mechanic Auto-mechaniker/in
apprenticeship Lehre, Ausbildung
own eigene/r/s
salon Friseursalon
to sound sich anhören
opportunity Möglichkeit, Gelegenheit
language Sprache
not … any more nicht mehr

Forget the interview!

A **Listen to the telephone dialogue. Tick the right pair of pictures (1–3).**
A1.14 Hören Sie sich den Telefondialog an. Machen Sie ein Häkchen an das passende Bildpaar (1–3).

1  ☐

2  ☐

3  ☐

B **Listen to the dialogue again. Tick A or B for sentences 1–4.**
Hören Sie sich den Dialog noch einmal an. Machen Sie bei den Sätzen 1–4 ein Häkchen bei A oder B.

1. A ☐ Peter's interview is on Thursday.
   B ☐ Peter's interview is on Friday.
2. A ☐ Peter is most awake in the morning.
   B ☐ Peter is most awake in the evening.
3. A ☐ Peter wants to wear jeans and a T-shirt.
   B ☐ Peter wants to wear a suit.
4. A ☐ Jenny Williams is an assistant.
   B ☐ Jenny Williams is the boss.

Grammar: Die Zukunftsformen von ***to be*** und ***have got*** → G 5

Clare is a student now. In the future she'll be an employee.
Clare ist jetzt Schülerin. In der Zukunft wird sie Angestellte sein.

I've got lots of time at the moment. Next year I'll have less time.
Im Moment habe ich viel Zeit. Nächstes Jahr werde ich weniger Zeit haben.

C **Everything will be different in the future. Finish the sentences. Use *will/'ll* and *won't* .**
In der Zukunft wird alles anders sein. Vervollständigen Sie die Sätze.
Benutzen Sie *will/'ll* und *won't* .

Example: → *Dana goes to school every day.* *In the future she won't go to school any more.*

1. We have to do lots of tests every month.
   In the future ______________________ to do tests any more.
2. Sam often doesn't get up before 11.
   In the future ______________________ up a lot earlier all the time!
3. At the moment Jenny goes out every night.
   In the future ______________________ out every night any more.
4. I haven't got a lot of money at the moment.
   In the future ______________________ lots of money!
5. There aren't many jobs for young people.
   In the future ______________________ more jobs.
6. At the moment Sergej has got a bike.
   In the future ______________________ a car!

to be awake
wach sein

suit
Anzug; Kostüm

A dream job?

Tarek Miller is 18. He lives in London with his parents. Tarek is looking for a job but he hasn't got any qualifications. On the internet he finds this job advert:

> **Mädchen (oder Junge) für alles gesucht!**
>
> German TV star in California is looking for a personal assistant to look after his two crazy children (10 + 12 years old, mother left us), cook (German food too!), drive everybody around and do many other jobs.
>
> Requirements: You should like children, speak English and German, be a good cook, have a clean driving licence – and always do what I tell you!
>
> Interested? Send application by email to: ▶ hans.german@staragency…com

Tarek is interested. On the internet he finds some ideas about how to write a job application. This is what he writes:

> Dear Mr German
>
> I saw your advert for a personal assistant online and I am now writing to apply for the position.
>
> I am sure that I have got all the necessary qualifications for this position:
> - I am very good at looking after crazy children because I was a crazy child myself.
> - My German isn't bad, and it will get better every day. I didn't have German at school, but I know more than just "Bayern München" and "Prost"! And I promise I will learn ten German words a day if I get the job.
> - Cooking is no problem. I do all the cooking at home already, usually canned soup. I am sure that I will quickly learn how to cook sauerkraut for you every day.
> - Chauffeur is my dream job. My driving licence will soon be clean again, and I promise I won't drink alcohol any more. (Have you got a Cadillac? I love Cadillacs!)
>
> It has always been my dream to work as a personal assistant and I've always wanted to see California, so the position that you offer is a great opportunity. I am living at home right now, thinking about my future, but I will be ready to start the job next month.
>
> I look forward to hearing from you. Of course I would gladly come to California for an interview. (Can I bring my mother too? I really hate flying.)
>
> Yours sincerely
> Tarek Miller

Vocabulary: **Rund um die Bewerbung**

(job) advert, apply, application, apprenticeship, (job) interview, look forward to hearing from …, opportunity, position, qualification, requirement

qualification Qualifikation; Voraussetzung

personal assistant persönliche/r Assistent/in

to look after betreuen

requirement Anforderung

application Bewerbung

how to write … wie man … schreibt

to apply (for) sich bewerben (um)

position (Arbeits-)Stelle

to promise versprechen

canned soup Suppe aus der Dose

chauffeur Chauffeur/in, Fahrer/in

alcohol Alkohol

to look forward to hearing from … sich darauf freuen, von … zu hören

I would ich würde

gladly gern

A **Finish the sentences. Write one or two English words.**
EXAM Vervollständigen Sie die Sätze. Schreiben Sie ein oder zwei englische Wörter.

Skills Tip

Lesen Sie jeden Satz in der Aufgabe gründlich durch. Machen Sie sich klar, was gefragt ist. Suchen Sie dann nach der passenden Stelle im Text und finden Sie die gewünschte Formulierung.

1 A German TV star is looking for a personal assistant for his home in ______.
2 Tarek Miller is interested in the job and writes an ______.
3 Tarek is sure that he has got the right ______ for the job.
4 Tarek does a lot of cooking. He and his parents often eat ______.
5 Tarek has a problem with planes. He doesn't like ______.

B **Give the opposite of the underlined word.**
EXAM Geben Sie das Gegenteil des unterstrichenen Wortes an.

1 drive <u>everybody</u> around ______
2 you should <u>like</u> children ______
3 be a <u>good</u> cook ______
4 it will get <u>better</u> ______

Grammar: Fragen, was in der Zukunft geschehen wird → G 5

Satzstellung: **Will you miss school next year?**
Wirst du die Schule nächstes Jahr vermissen?

C **Tarek's interview. Match the questions 1–4 to the answers A–F.**
EXAM **Two answers don't match.**
Tareks Bewerbungsgespräch. Ordnen Sie den Fragen 1–4 die Antworten A–F zu. Zwei Antworten passen nicht.

1 Will your German get better in the future?	A No, I didn't.
2 Did you learn German at school as a kid?	B No, I haven't.
3 Have you still got a drinking problem?	C No, I won't.
4 Is flying usually a problem for you?	D Yes, it is.
	E Yes, it will.
	F Yes, I was.

D **Circle the right word. The Grammar Box can help you.**
Umkringeln Sie das richtige Wort. Der *Grammar*-Kasten kann Ihnen helfen.

1 The German star: "Tarek is interesting. I think I'll give her / him a chance."
2 Tarek: "I'm so happy! The German star has invited me / you for an interview."
3 The star's children: "Hi Tarek! We're his crazy children. Do you like them / us ?"
4 Tarek: "My parents are great. I'll phone it / them every day from California."

Grammar: → G 13
Über jemanden oder etwas sprechen

I	you	he	she	it
me	you	him	her	it
we	you	they		
us	you	them		

Ziel: Ich kann Ratschläge erteilen.

The right clothes

A1.15 Leyla works in a clothes shop. She's good at helping customers.

Leyla	Good morning. How can I help you?
Customer	Hi. I'm looking for something special to wear. Hm, perhaps that short green dress over there?
Leyla	Sure, that'll suit you. Why don't you try it on?
Customer	I think it's a little short. What about this sexy pink top?
Leyla	Well, it depends. If you don't mind me asking – what do you need it for?
Customer	For my first job interview.
Leyla	What?! Well … I wouldn't recommend party clothes for a job interview.
Customer	But I don't want to spend money on things that I'll never wear again.
Leyla	You'll need some smart clothes in the job, too. Is it an office job?
Customer	Yes, it is. But I don't want to look like all the others.
Leyla	*You* won't – only your clothes! White blouse, blue suit. Here, I think you should try this. You'll be surprised.

A few minutes later …

Customer	Wow. You were right. It doesn't look bad at all.
Leyla	If I were you, I'd buy another blouse, perhaps a light blue one, so you can change the look.
Customer	OK. Fine. Thank you very much. If I get the job, I'll come here again – for some party clothes!

Vocabulary: Ratschläge erteilen

It depends.
I wouldn't recommend …
I think you should …
If I were you, I'd …
Why don't you …?

A **What is the dialogue about? Tick the right summary.**
Worum geht es in dem Dialog? Machen Sie ein Häkchen an die passende Zusammenfassung.

A ☐ Young woman explains right clothes for job interviews to shop assistant.
B ☐ Office worker tells young woman how to get office jobs.
C ☐ Shop assistant helps young woman to pick the right clothes.
D ☐ Young woman buys interesting party clothes with the help of an assistant.

B **Choose exercise 1 or 2.**
Wählen Sie Aufgabe 1 oder 2.

Vocabulary: Kleidung

blouse, coat, dress, leather shoes, shirt, skirt, suit, tie

1 **Finish the young woman's email.**
Vervollständigen Sie die Email der jungen Frau.

Hi Linda,

Yesterday I bought some really nice clothes for my ____________ [1]
next week. Luckily there was a very helpful ____________ [2].
I'll wear a blue ____________ [3] and a white ____________ [4]. I think it
looks really smart. So nothing can go wrong now – I'll get the ____________ [5] !

Love, Kirsty

2 **A young man comes into the shop. Write a similar dialogue to the one above.**
Ein junger Mann kommt in das Geschäft. Schreiben Sie einen ähnlichen Dialog wie den oben.

special besondere/r/s
to suit somebody jemandem gut stehen
to depend darauf ankommen
to recommend empfehlen
to spend ausgeben
smart schick
blouse Bluse
surprised überrascht
if I were you, I'd … an Ihrer Stelle würde ich …
look Aussehen
leather Leder
skirt Rock
tie Krawatte

Ziel: Ich kann ein Email-Bewerbungsschreiben formulieren.

C **Anna is looking for an interesting job in tourism. She finds an advert on the internet. Read the job advert.**
Anna sucht eine interessante Stelle im Tourismusbereich. Im Internet findet sie eine Anzeige. Lesen Sie die Stellenanzeige.

> **German/English Salesperson**
>
> *Tour Tanzania* are looking for German and English speaking salespeople for the safari business. Requirements: good computer skills, enthusiastic, good team player. Must be able to learn quickly. 23 – 35 years old. We will provide training.
>
> Applications in English with attached CV (pdf) to: ▶ paul.green@tourtanzania…com

D **Anna decides to apply for the job. Read her application letter. Then match the paragraphs 1 – 9 of Anna's email to the parts of an application letter (A – I) below.**
Anna beschließt, sich um die Stelle zu bewerben. Lesen Sie ihr Bewerbungsschreiben. Dann ordnen Sie die Absätze 1 – 9 von Annas Email den Teilen eines Bewerbungsschreibens (A – I) zu.

> Subject: Job application German/English Salesperson 1
>
> Dear Mr Green 2
>
> I am writing to apply for the position of German/English Salesperson as advertised on your website. 3
>
> As you can see from my attached CV, I am a German native speaker and I speak English almost fluently. I also have some experience working as a tour guide for Travel Tours in Germany. At the moment I am working for a travel agency, where I look after the computer bookings. 4
>
> The position that you are offering is just what I am looking for. I love working with people and I would like a job where I can use my English. 5
>
> My CV is attached. If you need more information on my qualifications, please let me know. 6
>
> I look forward to hearing from you. 7
>
> Yours sincerely 8
> Anna Bruckner 9
> Hauptstr. 16
> 45525 Hattingen
> Germany
> Home 0049 2324 4517…, Mobile 0049 172 3459933…
> anna_bruckner@speednet…de

1	C
2	
3	
4	
5	
6	
7	
8	
9	

A abschließender Gruß
B Anrede
C Betreffzeile
D Grund des Schreibens
E Hinweis auf Anlagen
F Hoffnung auf Antwort
G kurze Erläuterung der eigenen Fähigkeiten
H Name und alle Kontaktdaten
I persönliche Motivation

Grammar: Sagen, wie man etwas tut → G12

My English is fluent.	He's a terrible dancer.
I **speak** English fluent**ly**.	He **dances** terrib**ly**.

salesperson Verkaufs-angestellte/r
skill Fähigkeit, Fertigkeit
enthusiastic engagiert
to be a team player teamfähig sein
to be able in der Lage sein
to provide anbieten
training Schulung, Einarbeitung
attached beigefügt, angehängt
CV Lebenslauf
advertised ausgeschrieben
native speaker Mutter-sprachler/in
fluently fließend
experience Erfahrung
tour guide Reiseleiter/in
travel agency Reisebüro
booking Buchung

Great things will happen next year: Your parents will buy you a new car!

Grammar Check 1: *will-future (I'll find a job.)*

Kreuzen Sie die richtige Antwort an. Tragen Sie den Lösungsbuchstaben (nach dem Pfeil) unten auf der Seite ein.

1 Ich benutze das *will-future*, um zu sagen, was ich

A ☐ in der Vergangenheit gemacht habe. → E

B ☐ gerade mache. → P

C ☐ in der Zukunft machen werde. → U

2 Ich bilde das *will-future* mit *will* und der

A ☐ Grundform → R

B ☐ Gegenwartsform → L

C ☐ Vergangenheitsform → A

des Verbs.

3 In einem Satz mit *will-future* kann als Zeitangabe vorkommen:

A ☐ last year → N

B ☐ next year → E

C ☐ a year ago → I

In this job you'll travel a lot so you won't often use your office.

Grammar Check 2: *will-future* – Kurzformen

Kreuzen Sie die richtige Antwort an. Tragen Sie den Lösungsbuchstaben (nach dem Pfeil) unten auf der Seite ein.

4 Die Kurzform von *will* ist

A ☐ 'd → S

B ☐ 'll → R

C ☐ 's → T

5 Die Kurzform von *will not* ist

A ☐ wasn't → L

B ☐ weren't → S

C ☐ won't → D

There will be lots of jobs in the future. People will have more money.

Grammar Check 3: *will-future – to be* und *have got*

Kreuzen Sie die richtige Antwort an. Tragen Sie den Lösungsbuchstaben (nach dem Pfeil) unten auf der Seite ein.

6 Das *will-future* von *is* und *are* lautet

A ☐ will are → T

B ☐ will be → S

C ☐ will is → L

7 Das *will-future* von *have got* lautet

A ☐ will got → O

B ☐ will have → I

C ☐ will have got → A

I've got a surprise for them. Look. Do you like it?

Grammar Check 4: Über jemanden oder etwas sprechen

Kreuzen Sie die richtige Antwort an. Tragen Sie den Lösungsbuchstaben (nach dem Pfeil) unten auf der Seite ein.

8 Wenn ich über Personen sprechen will, benutze ich z.B.

A ☐ the → B

B ☐ them → P

C ☐ there → T

9 Wenn ich über einen Gegenstand oder eine Sache sprechen will, benutze ich z.B.

A ☐ him → C

B ☐ it → S

C ☐ me → F

Tragen Sie die Lösungsbuchstaben hier ein. Sind alle Fragen richtig gelöst, ergibt sich ein Wort aus dieser Unit.

9	1	4	8	2	7	6	3	5

Vocabulary Check 1: Wortpuzzle

Setzen Sie die englischen Wörter für die deutschen Begriffe aus den Einzelteilen in den drei Reihen zusammen. Dann tragen Sie die Lösungsbuchstaben (nach dem Pfeil am Wortende) weiter unten ein.

~~appren~~	ex	in	lan	op	po	qua	re
gua	lifi	peri	portu	quire	si	ter	~~tice~~
cation → R	ence → T	ge → A	nity → N	ment → G	~~ship~~ → N	tion → I	view → I

1 apprenticeship
Lehre, Ausbildung

2 ______
Möglichkeit, Gelegenheit

3 ______
Sprache

4 ______
Vorstellungsgespräch

5 ______
Qualifikation, Voraussetzung

6 ______
Anforderung

7 ______
(Arbeits-)Stelle

8 ______
Erfahrung

Lösungswort: 8 [ ] 5 [ ] 3 [ ] 7 [ ] 1 [N] 4 [ ] 2 [ ] 6 [ ]

Vocabulary Check 2: Synonyme (Wörter mit gleicher oder ähnlicher Bedeutung)

Finden Sie die passenden Synonyme zu den Wörtern 1–5. Tragen Sie dann die Lösungsbuchstaben (nach dem Pfeil) rechts ein.

get → S • job → U • promise → L • select → O • skill → T • smart → R • terrible → D • truck → N

1 position = ______
2 lorry = ______
3 awful = ______
4 receive = ______
5 pick = ______

Lösungswort: 4 [ ] 5 [ ] 1 [ ] 2 [ ] 3 [ ]

Video lounge

V5 BBC Motion Gallery

Tim gets a job

Read the questions and tick the right answer.
Lesen Sie die Fragen und machen Sie ein Häkchen an die passende Antwort.

1 Why does Tim apply for the job?
A ☐ He is bored with his old job.
B ☐ He hasn't got a job.

2 Why is the phone interview good news?
A ☐ It is easier than a personal interview.
B ☐ It means the people are interested in him.

A Playing basketball

EXAM Match the beginnings of the sentences (1–6) to the endings (A–F). Draw lines.

Skills Tip: Welche Verbform?

Zwei Überlegungen können Ihnen dabei helfen, die richtige Verbform zu finden:
- Die Frage danach, **wann** etwas stattfindet: Oft findet sich ein Signalwort (Zeitangabe) im Satz.
- Die Frage danach, **wie viele** Menschen handeln: Einzahl oder Mehrzahl?

1 Yesterday Tom …	A will play basketball.
2 Tomorrow Sue …	B are playing basketball.
3 At the moment Linda …	C play basketball.
4 Every day Jim …	D is playing basketball.
5 Right now, Tim and Lucy …	E played basketball.
6 Every Monday the children …	F plays basketball.

B Patty's decision

EXAM Fill in the correct form of the verbs in brackets.

1 Last year Patty ______________ **[left / leave / will leave]** school.

2 All of her friends ______________ **[had / have / has]** jobs today.

3 Only Patty ______________ **[was / is / will be]** still without a job now.

4 Yesterday she ______________ **[decided / decides / will decide]** to change that.

5 She ______________ **[wrote/writes/will write]** lots of applications tomorrow.

6 In the future she ______________ **[didn't waste / don't waste / won't waste]** any more time.

C The new job

EXAM Complete the sentences with the right English words for the German words in brackets. The box can help you.

I	you	he	she	it	we	you	they
me	you	him	her	it	us	you	them
my	your	his	her	its	our	your	their

1 My friend George is very happy about __________ **[seinen]** new job.

2 He applied for __________ **[ihn]** immediately after __________ **[er]** saw the advert online.

3 He wanted my sister's help with the application, so he told __________ **[ihr]** about the advert.

4 __________ **[sie]** gave __________ **[ihm]** some good advice.

5 When his parents heard about the job, __________ **[sie]** became angry with __________ **[ihn]**.

6 George called __________ **[mich]** and I had to explain to __________ **[ihnen]** that DJ really isn't such a bad job.

decision Entscheidung
to leave verlassen
to decide (sich) entscheiden
to waste verschwenden
immediately sofort

D The fast food restaurant

EXAM

Fill in the correct English words.

1 When the new fast food restaurant needed employees, not ____________ [viele] people applied.

2 Everybody thought that the restaurant paid less money ____________ [als] other firms.

3 So all of the people ____________ [die] applied got a job at the restaurant.

4 They all love ____________ [ihre] jobs.

5 They think that they have got ____________ [die besten] jobs in town!

E The application

Mary needs money for her singing lessons. So she wants to apply for a job as an au pair girl in France. Look at her notes for the application and circle the right word.

1 At the moment I can only speak English, but I'll learn to speak French [dangerously] [fluently].

2 I know how to clean a house. I'll clean your house [badly] [beautifully].

3 I'm a very patient girl. I promise that I won't talk to the children [angrily] [easily].

4 I'm not a very good cook, but I won't cook [carefully] [terribly].

5 Everybody says I'm nice. I'll always talk to your guests [boringly] [politely].

6 I'll have to practise my singing every day, but you don't have to worry: I'll always sing [cheaply] [quietly].

F My future

Read the notes. They are in the right order. Then put in the missing words and make sentences.

1 [in about ten years] [I'll be] [rich man]

____.

2 [have] [big car] [big house] [big family]

____.

3 [won't have to work a lot because] [have employees]

____.

4 [be away often because] [have lots of free time]

____.

5 [want to be] [famous pop star]

____.

note Notiz

patient geduldig

guest Gast

to practise üben

Textarbeit: Matching

A1.25

My teacher changed my life

"When I was fifteen my mother died and I felt that my dreams were over," Arlene Phillips remembers. "I wanted to become a professional dancer in London but I had a brother and a sister and we had to look after our house and my father. However, I continued my dancing course. When I finished it my teacher there asked me to be a dance teacher. In this way I could earn some money to help my family.

One day she sent me to a dancing course in London which would help me to become a better teacher. I had only been to London once and I was really excited. While I was doing my course there I looked through a classroom door and I saw a class in modern American jazz dance. It was different to anything I had ever seen and I knew that was what I wanted to do. I couldn't go home again.

I went to Molly, the teacher of the class, and told her my story and she said: "Come and stay in my flat." I rang home. My family wasn't happy, of course. And my dance teacher in my home town was really upset when I told her I was going to stay in London.

It wasn't all fun there. Dance lessons are expensive, so I had to do many different jobs to make enough money. I had to practise very hard in my lessons and sometimes my dance teacher made me feel that I would never be good enough. So I worked even harder.

Today she's proud of me and I'll never forget what she did for me!" (276 words)

Annotations:
line 4 **professional** – Berufs-/Profi-
line 6 **however** – jedoch
line 25 **upset** – aufgebracht, bestürzt
line 31 **to practise** – üben

Skills Tip: ***Matching*** **= Zuordnung**

- Sie lesen einen **Satzanfang** und müssen das passende **Satzende** dazu finden.
- **Wichtig:** Zwei Satzenden lassen sich **nicht** zuordnen!
- Bei *Matching* ist besonders wichtig, dass der neue Satz **inhaltlich** zum Text passt.
- Wenn Sie sich bei einer Aufgabe nicht entscheiden können, schreiben Sie sich die möglichen Satzenden an den Rand. Was ergibt am meisten Sinn? Vergleichen Sie das Ergebnis mit dem Text.

Match the beginnings 1–5 to five of the endings A–G according to the text. Two endings do not match.

☐ 1 **When her mother died …**
☐ 2 Arlene still went to her dancing course and then …
☐ 3 She wanted to be a better dance teacher so …
☐ 4 Modern dance was so exciting that …
☐ 5 Arlene thought that she was not good enough as a professional dancer so …

A … she left London.
B … Arlene decided to stay in London.
C … **Arlene had to look after their house and father.**
D … she practised more.
E … Arlene did her first dancing course in London.
F … she became a dance teacher.
G … Arlene was very proud.

Managing Situations: Guided composition

Skills Tip: ***Guided composition*** **bedeutet Schreiben mit Hilfestellung.**

- Sie schreiben z. B. einen **Brief** oder eine Email über ein bestimmtes Thema.
- Lesen Sie die Situationsbeschreibung gründlich durch. **Wichtig: An wen** (Freund/in oder fremde Person) soll sich Ihr Schreiben richten? **Aus welchem Anlass** verfassen Sie das Schreiben? **Worüber** sollen Sie schreiben?
- Strukturieren Sie Ihren Text, indem Sie die vorgegebenen Punkte aufgreifen.
- **Anfang und Ende** des Textes sind immer vorgegeben.

You are practising **job applications**. In a test you have to write a short **letter to an English company**. Tell them **about yourself**.

Write about 50 words in complete English sentences, please. Tell them:

- your name
- your age
- where you live
- your hobbies
- your best subjects
- where you would like to work
- what kind of work you would like to do
- your plans for the future

Dear Sir or Madam

My name is ______________________________

____

____

____

____

____

____

____

____

____

Yours faithfully

____

uz76gm

6 On the job

Ziel: Ich kann sagen, was gerade (oder noch nicht) geschehen ist und was ich schon einmal (oder noch nie) getan habe. *Beispiel: I've just found a new job in a salon. But I've never worked as a hairdresser before! (present perfect)*

A **Nick and Liana. Read the statements.**
Nick und Liana. Lesen Sie die Aussagen.

Hi. My name is Nick.
I'm a car mechanic.
I've just repaired another car.

My dream is to work as a racing mechanic one day.

I've done some racing before.

But I've never touched a Formula One car before.

I know that I'll need lots of experience for the job.

Hi. I'm Liana.
I'm a gardener.
I've just planted some tomatoes.

I dream of having my own flower shop one day.

I've worked as a florist before.

But I've never had a shop before.

I know that I'll have to save a lot of money.

What are Nick and Liana talking about? Tick the right answer.
Worüber sprechen Nick und Liana? Machen Sie ein Häkchen an die richtige Antwort.

Nick and Liana are talking about ...

- **A** ☐ their hobbies and their jobs.
- **B** ☐ their applications and their jobs.
- **C** ☐ their jobs and their career dreams.
- **D** ☐ their friends and their career dreams.

before zuvor, schon einmal
racing (Motor-)Rennen
to touch berühren
Formula One Formel Eins
gardener Gärtner/in
to plant (ein)pflanzen
florist Florist/in
to save sparen
career dream Berufstraum
to serve bedienen; servieren

Vocabulary: Berufliche Tätigkeiten

cook meals, drive trucks, paint houses, plant flowers, repair cars, serve customers, write emails

Grammar: Was gerade / noch nicht / schon einmal / noch nie geschehen ist → **G 4**

regelmäßige Verben:
have (Kurzform **'ve**) oder **has** + **Verb** + **-ed**

I've just repaired a car.
Ich habe soeben ein Auto repariert.

Has Tom worked as a mechanic before?
Hat Tom schon einmal als Mechaniker gearbeitet?

unregelmäßige Verben:
have (Kurzform **'ve**) oder **has** + **Verb**
(Formen → vordere Umschlagseite, innen)

Leah hasn't written her application yet.
Leah hat ihre Bewerbung noch nicht geschrieben.

I've never been to a car race before.
Ich bin noch nie bei einem Autorennen gewesen.

B **What about you?**
Und Sie?

I've worked as a / I've ______________________ before.

____

Ask Aysha

A **Listen to the radio show. What jobs do the three callers want to do? Tick the right three pictures.**
A1.16 Hören Sie sich die Radiosendung an. Welche Berufe wollen die drei Anrufenden ausüben? Machen Sie ein Häkchen an die drei passenden Bilder.

1

2
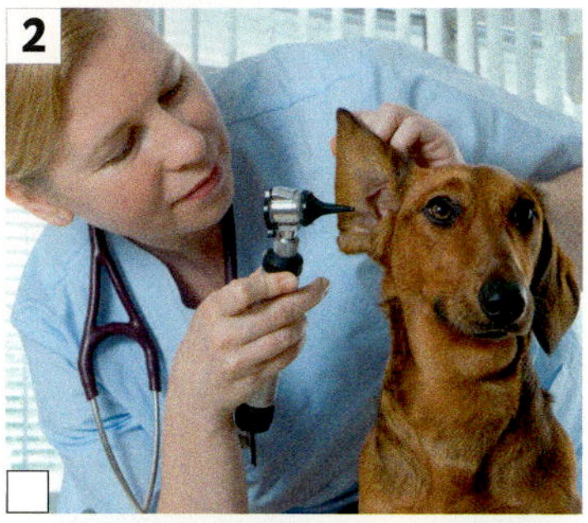

3

4

5

6

B **Listen to the radio show again. Tick *true* or *false* for sentences 1–4.**
Hören Sie sich die Radiosendung noch einmal an. Machen Sie bei den Sätzen 1–4 ein Häkchen bei *richtig* oder *falsch*.

	true	false
1 Sally is interested in cars and wants to work in the office of a garage.	☐	☐
2 Greg left school a few months ago and watches TV a lot.	☐	☐
3 Paula can't cook, but she wants to be a chef.	☐	☐
4 People phone Aysha because she gives them advice.	☐	☐

C **On the job. Finish the sentences with the right verb.**
Bei der Arbeit. Vervollständigen Sie die Sätze mit dem richtigen Verb.

cooked • driven • finished • painted • planted • repaired • served • told

1 "Murat, why haven't you cooked the chicken soup yet?"
– "Because I've never ______________________ chicken soup before!"

2 "Jess, why aren't you painting that wall over there?"
– "Because I haven't ______________________ this wall here yet!"

3 "Karel, have you ______________________ Mr Lee's car?"
– "Yes, I've just finished it, boss."

4 "Has Aida ______________________ the flowers?"
– "I'm not sure, boss. I'll ask her."

5 "Have you ______________________ a truck before, Susan?"
– "Of course I have! I've got a truck licence, boss."

a few months ago
vor ein paar Monaten

chef
Koch/Köchin

wall
Wand, Mauer

A1.17

Dirty hands

Monday. Another day at Newtown Motors. Another day trying to sell a car. Simon dealt with lots of emails, opened doors, offered and served coffee, took some terrible drivers for test drives – but he didn't sell a single car.

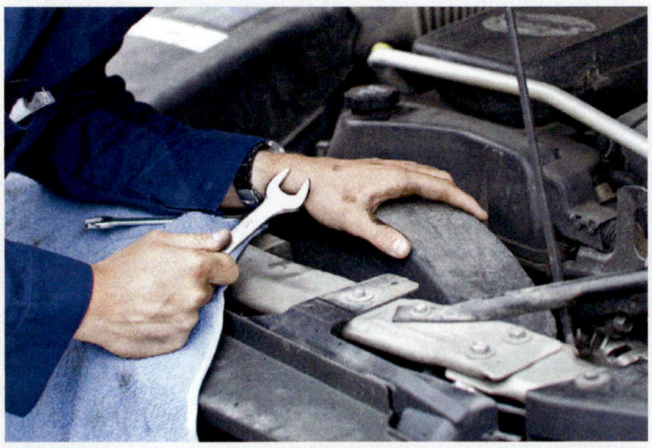

In the evening he drove home in his own car. He thought back to that important conversation with his boss, Mrs Grant. It was three months ago, before he became one of her car salesmen, but it felt like yesterday …

Mrs Grant Well, Simon, let me tell you that we're very pleased with your work. We've never had such a good mechanic before. Last week, for example, Mr Fenton's van – you found out what was wrong with it in five minutes.

Simon That's my job, Mrs Grant. I've always been good at repairing things. And I like helping people with their cars. I'm happy when the customers are happy.

Mrs Grant And that's why I'm talking to you today, Simon. Our best salesman has just left us. I've decided to offer the job to our friendliest employee – you.

Simon That's very nice of you, Mrs Grant, but I really like working on the cars. I've never thought about selling cars before and …

Mrs Grant … and you'll love the job. You're good with people, you're polite – and you won't have dirty hands any more! I'm sure your wife will be happy about that.

No more dirty hands. That was true. But he missed talking to the other mechanics, he missed trying to find the problem with an engine and helping car drivers. Now Simon had to tell people to give up their old car and buy a new one. He even had to wear a suit!

At home Simon talked to his wife.

"You look happy," Julie, his wife, said. "Wait – you look like you've just sold a car."

"No, I haven't," Simon answered. "I'll never sell a car."

"What?" Julie didn't understand.

"My three months probation is almost over – and I've just decided what to do," said Simon. "Next week I'll tell Mrs Grant that I really don't want to be a salesman. I want to repair cars again. That's what I'm good at. That's what I'm happy with. I'm so glad I haven't really said 'yes' yet. And I hope you won't mind the dirty hands again."

"But I've always loved your dirty hands, darling," Julie said. "I married a car mechanic, remember, not a salesman!"

to deal with sich kümmern um
test drive Probefahrt
single einzig
conversation Gespräch
to become werden
car salesman Autoverkäufer
pleased zufrieden
such a … so ein/e/en …
that's why deshalb
to decide (sich) entscheiden
wife Ehefrau
to miss vermissen
engine Motor; Maschine
even sogar
probation Probezeit
over vorbei
glad froh
to marry heiraten

Vocabulary: Was auf der Arbeit zu tun ist

mit Dingen: check something, deal with something, find out something, organize something, plan something, present something, recommend something, translate something, work on something
mit Menschen: drive somebody, help somebody, listen to somebody, look after somebody, meet somebody, phone somebody, talk to somebody, tell somebody, thank somebody

A EXAM **Match the beginnings 1–5 to the endings A–E.**
Ordnen Sie den Satzanfängen 1–5 die Satzenden A–E zu.

Skills Tip

Lesen Sie alle Satzenden gründlich durch, bevor Sie das passende Ende zum jeweiligen Satzanfang aussuchen. Wichtig: Der neue Satz muss **inhaltlich** zum Text links passen!

1 Simon Marples became a car salesman three months ago, after …
2 But Simon was a car mechanic and …
3 As a salesman Simon didn't have dirty hands anymore but …
4 Simon had to tell people to buy a new car when …
5 When the probation was over, …

A … he really loved his job.
B … Simon decided to be a car mechanic again.
C … his boss offered him the job.
D … he really wanted to repair their old car.
E … he had to wear a suit.

B **Who is talking – Simon, Julie, Mrs Grant or Mr Fenton (a customer)? Write the name behind the statement.**
Wer spricht – Simon, Julie, Mrs Grant oder Mr Fenton (ein Kunde)? Schreiben Sie den Namen hinter die Aussage.

1 "Every man should have clean hands – always." ____________
2 "I'm so glad that I don't have to buy a new van yet." ____________
3 "It's so good to see you happy again!" ____________
4 "Don't worry. I'm sure we'll be able to repair it." ____________

C EXAM **Find a synonym for the underlined word. The words that you need are in the text.**
Finden Sie ein Synonym für das unterstrichene Wort. Die Wörter, die Sie brauchen, befinden sich im Text.

Skills Tip

Synonyme sind Wörter mit gleicher Bedeutung (wie „toll" und „super"). In der Übung reichen aber auch Wörter mit einer ähnlichen Bedeutung (wie „freundlich" und „höflich").

1 very bad drivers ____________
2 we're very happy ____________
3 you're friendly ____________

Grammar: ***many*** **(= viele) und** ***much*** **(= viel)**

I always get too many emails.
Ich bekomme immer zu viele Emails.

I don't have much time.
Ich habe nicht viel Zeit.

D **Simon's job. Circle the right word.**
Simons Job. Umkringeln Sie das richtige Wort.

1 How many | much money do you want to spend on your new car?
2 Well, I'm new in this job. I haven't sold many | much cars yet.
3 Not many | much customers really want to buy a car. They just want to go for a test drive.
4 Working as a salesman isn't many | much fun for me. I want to work as a mechanic again.

Ziel: Ich kann meine Meinung sagen und Vorschläge machen.

My problem at work

Samantha Hobart has got a problem. She discusses it with her social network friends.

Samantha Hobart I started my first real hairdressing job at CheapCuts Salon last week and I love it! But: Every time I sit down to have my lunch break, one of my colleagues tells me to continue working because there's so much to do. I think that's wrong. What do you think?
5 hours ago Like Comment

Luke Middleton I really don't think that's OK. You could complain to the boss. Perhaps the salon needs more hairdressers. Why don't you discuss it with her?
4 hours ago Like

Helen McGregor I agree with Luke. I know that every full-time employee has a right to a lunch break.
4 hours ago Like

Sally Brown I don't agree with Luke and Helen. If you want to stay at the salon, you should keep your mouth shut and work.
3 hours ago Like

Jake Parsons I think Sally is right because breaks are a waste of time. Who needs food anyway? Remember: You can never be *too* thin, ha, ha!
2 hours ago Like

A **Who says what? Tick the right answers.**
Wer sagt was? Machen Sie ein Häkchen an die richtigen Antworten.

	Luke	Helen	Sally	Jake
1 Samantha thinks what happens to her is wrong. Who agrees?	☐	☐	☐	☐
2 Who has ideas about what Samantha should do?	☐	☐	☐	☐
3 Who writes the least serious entry?	☐	☐	☐	☐
4 Who has an idea that could be interesting for the boss?	☐	☐	☐	☐

Vocabulary: Die eigene Meinung sagen und Vorschläge machen

Meinungen äußern: I (don't) think …
Auf andere Meinungen reagieren: I (don't) agree … / … is / are right / wrong.
Begründungen geben: … because …
Vorschläge machen: Perhaps … / Why don't you …? / You could … / You should …

B **Choose exercise 1 or 2.**
Wählen Sie Aufgabe 1 oder 2.

1 **Match the entries 1–3 and the (not very serious) comments A–C.**
Ordnen Sie den Einträgen 1–3 die (nicht sehr ernst gemeinten) Kommentare A–C zu.

1 My colleagues shout at me.
2 I haven't got enough money.
3 I'm never allowed to drive the firm's car.

A You could get a driving licence.
B Why don't you get a job?
C Perhaps you shouldn't wear earphones at work.

2 **You are one of Samantha's social network friends. Write the next comment.**
Sie sind eine/r von Samanthas Freunden/Freundinnnen in diesem sozialen Netzwerk. Schreiben Sie den nächsten Kommentar.

to discuss diskutieren
to continue working weiter arbeiten
to complain sich beschweren
to agree zustimmen
full-time Ganztags-
right Recht
to keep your mouth shut den Mund halten
a waste of time Zeitverschwendung
anyway überhaupt
thin dünn
least serious am wenigsten ernst gemeint

Ziel: Ich kann über Firmenbereiche und die nötigen Anforderungen dafür sprechen.

Where do they work?

A **Read statements 1–10 and match the English words for the parts of a firm to the German words A–J.**
Lesen Sie die Aussagen 1–10 und ordnen Sie den englischen Wörtern für Firmenbereiche die deutschen Wörter A–J zu.

1 I'm good with my hands and I want to produce things so I work in **production**.	C	A EDV-Abteilung
2 I'm good at drawing technical things. That's why I work in **design**.	____	B Empfang
3 I'm interested in computer work. I work in **IT**.	____	C Fertigung
4 I've always been good at selling things to people so I work in **sales**.	____	D Kantine
5 I'm good with words and I like writing so I love working in **publicity**.	____	E Konstruktion
6 I like office work but I also like to deal with people. I work in **human resources**.	____	F Kundendienst
7 I'm polite and I'm good at talking to people. I work in the **reception**.	____	G Personalabteilung
8 I like sorting things and I don't like sitting around so I work in the **post room**.	____	H Poststelle
9 I like people and I'm a very patient person. That's why I work in **customer services**.	____	I Vertrieb
10 I like eating – so I'm happy working in the **canteen**!	____	J Werbung

B **Luke is taking a group of pupils on a tour of the firm.**
Put in the parts of the firm that he is describing.
Luke macht mit einer Schülergruppe einen Rundgang durch die Firma. Fügen Sie die Firmenbereiche ein, die er beschreibt.

Good morning and welcome to our tour of the firm. We start with the biggest place here. It's where everything is produced, so it's called ______________________ [1]. Next we'll have a quick look at the room where all the new technical things are drawn. It's called ______________________ [2]. There isn't much to see in all the offices. Here, for example, is the office where our adverts are written. We call this part of the firm ______________________ [3]. And next you can have a look at the ______________________ [4] where all our many letters and parcels are sorted. And you'll all love the following place. Are you hungry? It's where our meals are cooked – the ______________________ [5]!

to produce herstellen, produzieren
to draw zeichnen
technical technisch
to sort sortieren
patient geduldig
welcome willkommen
parcel Paket

Grammar: Sagen, was getan wird → G 8

An advert **is written**.	Letters **are sorted**.
Eine Anzeige wird geschrieben.	Briefe werden sortiert.

Grammar Check 1: *present perfect (I've just found a new job.)*

Kreuzen Sie die richtige Antwort an. Tragen Sie den Lösungsbuchstaben (nach dem Pfeil) unten auf der Seite ein.

1 Ich benutze das *present perfect*, um zu sagen, was ich

A ☐ gerade gemacht habe. → E

B ☐ gerade mache. → A

C ☐ in der Zukunft machen werde. → R

2 Ich benutze das *present perfect* auch, um zu sagen, was ich

A ☐ schon einmal gemacht habe. → E

B ☐ ständig mache. → I

C ☐ nie machen werde. → R

3 In einem Satz mit *present perfect* kann als Zeitangabe vorkommen:

A ☐ at the moment → R

B ☐ just → L

C ☐ next year → E

4 Ich bilde das *present perfect* mit *have/has* und einem regelmäßigen Verb +

A ☐ -ed → A

B ☐ -ing → R

C ☐ -s → E

oder einem unregelmäßigen Verb.

Grammar Check 2: *much* und *many*

Kreuzen Sie die richtige Antwort an. Tragen Sie den Lösungsbuchstaben (nach dem Pfeil) unten auf der Seite ein.

5 Wenn ich über **viele** (einzelne) Dinge oder Menschen sprechen will, benutze ich

A ☐ many → S

B ☐ much → T

C ☐ some → R

6 Wenn ich sagen will, dass ich nicht **viel** Zeit/Geld usw. habe, benutze ich

A ☐ many → S

B ☐ most → B

C ☐ much → P

Tragen Sie die Lösungsbuchstaben hier ein. Sind alle Fragen richtig gelöst, ergibt sich ein Wort aus dieser Unit.

6	3	2	4	5	1	
						D

Vocabulary Check 1: Suchworträtsel

Finden Sie 12 Wörter aus diesem Buch (waagerecht und senkrecht).

A	N	T	Y	P	R	O	R	W	E	N	K	M	O	P	L	T
R	C	H	A	U	F	F	E	U	R	I	S	C	I	E	F	E
M	U	L	D	P	A	R	P	G	U	A	W	I	N	T	S	Y
E	M	M	O	N	O	C	O	L	L	E	A	G	U	E	I	C
C	H	R	O	E	I	N	R	A	U	M	D	I	N	G	A	L
H	O	U	N	I	T	E	T	R	G	U	B	S	T	O	R	A
A	N	S	H	G	T	D	E	M	A	G	O	T	O	O	N	S
N	E	T	T	H	A	I	R	D	R	E	S	S	E	R	T	S
I	F	M	U	B	S	F	D	I	D	A	S	L	I	N	T	M
C	U	S	T	O	M	E	R	Z	E	N	I	C	K	W	E	A
O	D	L	B	U	A	X	L	H	N	B	G	O	R	A	T	T
R	O	I	F	R	I	E	N	D	E	M	P	L	O	Y	E	E
T	R	A	G	H	R	S	T	I	R	Y	E	S	S	A	L	W

Tipp: Es sind alles Wörter für Personen.
5 Wörter sind Berufsbezeichnungen.
4 Wörter sind Bezeichnungen für Menschen am Arbeitsplatz.
3 Wörter sind andere Bezeichnungen für Menschen, die Sie kennen.

Vocabulary Check 2: Verben

Gesucht werden neue englische Verben aus dieser Unit. Das markierte Lösungswort, von oben nach unten gelesen, ergibt ein weiteres Verb.

1 berühren: ☐☐☐☐☐
2 werden: ☐☐☐☐☐☐
3 vermissen: ☐☐☐☐
4 herstellen, produzieren: ☐☐☐☐☐☐☐
L
5 zustimmen: ☐☐☐☐☐
6 diskutieren: ☐☐☐☐☐☐☐
7 (ein)pflanzen: ☐☐☐☐☐

Video lounge

V6 | BBC Motion Gallery

London and the Tube

Tick the right summary.
Machen Sie ein Häkchen an die passende Zusammenfassung.

A ☐ The Tube is a London underground station. It's always busy. You have to stop the trains to do repairs.

B ☐ The Tube is the name for a special team of repairmen in London. They put in new tracks at midnight.

C ☐ The Tube is the London underground train system. It's very old. It can only be repaired at night.

A Irregular verbs
Put in the missing forms of the irregular verbs. (→ vordere Umschlagseite, innen)

1 become – became – ______
2 bet – ______ – bet
3 deal – dealt – ______
4 ______ – did – done
5 draw – ______ – drawn
6 ______ – flew – flown
7 go – went – ______
8 have – had – ______
9 make – ______ – made
10 ______ – wrote – written

B Looking for a job
Pick the right word and finish the sentences.

before • just • never • yet

1 Tina has ______ sent her application for a job as a saleswoman to Newtown Motors.
2 She hopes that she'll get the job but she has ______ sold a car before.
3 What if there's an interview soon? I haven't bought any smart clothes ______!
4 And what if they ask me: "Have you worked as a saleswoman ______?"

C My first interview
Circle the right word.

1 I'm so excited! I've never been in | to a job interview before.
2 Some from | of my friends haven't even written applications yet.
3 I'm really interested in | of dealing with people.
4 And I think that I'm good at | in organizing.
5 A teacher from | to my old school said I should be a doctor's assistant.
6 So I applied of | to a big medical centre in town and they've just invited me!

D At Newtown Motors
EXAM Match the beginnings and the endings of the sentences. Draw lines.

1 Simon, the new salesman, hasn't sold …
2 I don't think that he's having …
3 But he's really good with …
4 Yes, those customers who don't want to spend …
5 Well, have you noticed that not …
6 Yes, I have. So let's look at …

A much money on a new car!
B some of the customers.
C some of the new applications now.
D many cars yet.
E much fun in his new job.
F many cars are repaired any more?

E My job

EXAM

Fill in the correct English words.

1 ______________ [Als] a receptionist for a big firm, I always have to be very friendly.

2 ______________ [Viele] people come through the door or phone the firm every day.

3 I have to politely find out how I can help ______________ [ihnen].

4 Receptionists have to be ______________ [besser] than other people at organizing.

5 And it helps if they know ______________ [die meisten] of their colleagues personally!

F Discount week at Newtown Motors

Discount week at Newtown Motors is over. Simon is telling Julie what happened. Finish the sentences with *was* or *were*.

1 Last week a 10% discount ______________ given on used cars.

2 First adverts ______________ put in the local papers.

3 When customers came to look at cars, coffee ______________ offered to them.

4 Some interested drivers ______________ taken for test drives.

5 Even the mechanics ______________ asked to help.

6 In the end, many cars ______________ sold.

G Patrick, the chef

Read the German notes and make full English sentences. (If you need help, look at page 66.)

Hi. My name is Patrick. I'm a chef.

1 habe gerade ein Essen für die Angestellten gekocht

I've ______________________________

______________________________.

2 Traum: eines Tages eigenes Restaurant haben

____

______________________________.

3 habe schon einmal in einem Hotel gekocht

____

______________________________.

4 aber habe noch nie ein Restaurant gehabt

____

______________________________.

5 weiß, dass ich viel Erfahrung und Geld brauchen werde

____

______________________________.

Textarbeit: Aussagen über den Text, Vocabulary work, Grammar

A1.26

Work and travel

"Even if you don't have a lot of money, you can travel to far-away countries," says nineteen-year-old Sue from Wales. "Last year I went to New Zealand for three months. I had saved some money for the plane ticket but I didn't have enough for a long stay. That is why I decided to work there in my holidays. I had already found a lot of information about work and travel in New Zealand on the internet and had some addresses.

For the first two weeks I helped to pick kiwi fruit. It was hard work and I had to share a room with three other girls. But it was quite interesting because there were so many young people from all over the world," Sue says.

"I made friends there with one of my room mates and we decided to travel together. New Zealand is really beautiful. We usually walked or took the train and we spent the nights in youth hostels, which are not too expensive. After a while we had to earn some money again and we found a job at a hotel where we helped to clean the rooms. The pay was not bad and we were able to travel again soon. Work and travel is really a good idea for young people. I hope that I can do this again next year – I think Australia would be a good idea."

Today several organizations in New Zealand have specialized in "working holidays" for young people, who can get working visas for a year or two. Then they are allowed to earn money and to work in the country. You can even get a visa online. (281 words)

Annotations:
line 12 **to pick** – pflücken
line 32 **to specialize in** – sich spezialisieren auf
line 33 **visa** – Visum, Einreisegenehmigung

A Aussagen über den Text

Entscheiden Sie, ob die Aussagen richtig oder falsch sind.
Notieren Sie Ihre Antwort hinter der Aussage.

	Aussage	
1	Sue arbeitete während ihres Urlaubs im letzten Jahr.	
2	Die Informationen über Neuseeland erhielt Sue von ihren Eltern.	
3	Während Sue half, Kiwis zu pflücken, hatte sie kein eigenes Zimmer für sich.	
4	Normalerweise übernachtete Sue in Hotels.	
5	Junge Leute können ein Visum für Neuseeland bekommen, um dort zu reisen und zu arbeiten	
	Statement	
6	Sue is from New Zealand.	
7	Sue went on holiday for three months last year.	
8	Sue had the money to buy a plane ticket.	
9	Sue met a boy and travelled together with him.	
10	Sue had different jobs in New Zealand.	

B Vocabulary work

Find the word **in the text** for …

1 a person who lives in a room together with another person: ______

2 a continent: ______

Give the **opposite**:

3 long (line 6) ______

4 some (line 10) ______

5 expensive (line 23) ______

C Grammar

1 Fill in the **correct form of the verbs** in brackets.

Last year Sue ______ **[has gone / went / goes]** to New Zealand.
She ______ **[not had / does not have / did not have]** enough money then so
she ______ **[has / had / have]** to work there.
Now she ______ **[plans / planning / is planning]** her next trip to Australia.
She ______ **[would like / likes / liked]** to stay there for two months.

2 Fill in the **correct English words**.

Sue ______ **[wirklich]** loves New Zealand. She thinks it is ______ **[schöner]**
than ______ **[viele]** other countries. Next year she is going to Australia
______ **[das / welches]** is ______ **[genauso schön wie]**
New Zealand.

t96aj7

7 Let's go!

Ziel: Ich kann Pläne und Absichten formulieren. *Beispiel: I'm going to find a new job. (going to-future)*

A After school. Read the dialogue.
Nach der Schule. Lesen Sie das Gespräch.

1. Hi Tarik. School is almost over. What are you going to do after school?

Hi Kate. I'm going to drive a truck through Europe in the summer. After that – who knows? What about you two?

2. Leo and I are going to go to Sweden for a few months.

Really? Cool. What are you going to do there?

3. I'm going to work in a restaurant and Leo is going to work as a builder.

But you don't speak Swedish, do you?

4. No, but they said that it's OK if we speak English. I'm really excited. I've always wanted to go abroad for a while.

Yeah, well … But why Sweden?

5. Leo's parents have English friends there. They helped us find the jobs.

Oh, I see. Yeah, sounds good. I'm going to be in Spain a lot – in the truck, of course.

6. That sounds good too. Listen, Tarik, have fun. Let's keep in touch, OK?

Yeah, sure. Say hi to Leo from me. And if I come to Sweden, I'll give you a call!

over vorbei
through durch
Europe Europa
Sweden Schweden
builder Bauarbeiter/in
Swedish Schwedisch
excited aufgeregt
abroad im/ins Ausland
while Weile
to keep in touch in Kontakt bleiben
Say hi to … from me. Grüße … von mir.
to give somebody a call jemanden anrufen

What's true? Tick the right statements.
Was stimmt? Machen Sie ein Häkchen an die richtigen Aussagen.

A ☐ Tarik and Kate are colleagues.
B ☐ Tarik is going to work as a driver.
C ☐ Kate is going to go abroad.
D ☐ Kate is going to live alone.
E ☐ Kate speaks Swedish.
F ☐ Tarik is going to drive a truck to Spain.

Vocabulary: Im Gespräch reagieren

I see. – Listen, … – Really?
Sure. – That sounds good.
What about …? – Yeah, well …

Grammar: Pläne und Absichten → G 6

I'm going to work as a hairdresser.
Ich werde als Friseur/in arbeiten.
Sue is going to go abroad.
Sue hat vor, ins Ausland zu gehen.

B What about you?
Und Sie?

I'm going to be a ______________________.

I'd like to work in ______________________.

Poland

Croatia

Italy

Lithuania

Slovenia

Portugal

Going abroad for work

A Listen to the phone call. What are Nils and Sandra talking about? Tick the three right pictures.
A1.18 Hören Sie sich das Telefongespräch an. Worüber unterhalten sich Nils und Sandra? Machen Sie ein Häkchen an die drei passenden Bilder.

1  ☐
2  ☐
3  ☐
4  ☐
5  ☐

B Listen to the phone call again. Tick A, B or C for sentences 1–4.
Hören Sie sich das Telefongespräch noch einmal an. Machen Sie bei den Sätzen 1–4 ein Häkchen bei A, B oder C.

1 **Nils is starting a new job in**
- A ☐ Germany.
- B ☐ England.
- C ☐ Italy.

2 **Nils is going to work**
- A ☐ on a ship.
- B ☐ as a driver.
- C ☐ in a restaurant.

3 **Sandra tells Nils to**
- A ☐ plan a meal.
- B ☐ drive carefully.
- C ☐ have breakfast first.

4 **Nils' first day in the new job is**
- A ☐ today.
- B ☐ tomorrow.
- C ☐ on Monday.

C Plans. Choose the right verb and circle it.
Pläne. Wählen Sie das richtige Verb und umkringeln Sie es.

1 First Nils is going to [find] [go] [look] his new colleagues in the restaurant.
2 Then Sandra is going to [draw] [rent] [show] him his new flat.
3 They're all going to [have] [like] [recommend] a meal together after the guests have left.
4 Nils is going to [explain] [say] [tell] them about his plans for the next week.

Grammar: Bedingungssätze → G 9

If I get the new job, I'll earn / I won't earn more money.
Wenn ich die neue Stelle bekomme, verdiene ich (nicht) mehr Geld.

D What if ...? Finish the if-sentences. Use *will/'ll* ☺ and *won't* ☹.
Was ist, wenn ...? Vervollständigen Sie die if-Sätze. Benutzen Sie *will/'ll* ☺ und *won't* ☹.

1 I like going to other countries.
☺ If I find a job abroad, I ______________ leave Germany.

2 An English firm has offered me a job.
☺ If I take it, they ______________ even pay for my flat there.

3 Pat's boyfriend is looking for a job abroad.
☺ If he gets one, Pat ______________ go with him.

4 I'm glad that I can speak English.
☹ If I need a holiday job abroad, I ______________ have problems finding one.

Italy
Italien

guest
Gast

A 1.19

Immigrants are important to our town

by Rebecca Carter

If you come to our town, you won't really notice them. But without immigrants, life here would be quite different – and not half as nice! Rebecca Carter talked to four of them.

Bina Dinkar is a chef at the "Taj Mahal" Indian restaurant. She came to England 30 years ago, as a baby. "I'm not going to leave this town. It's my home," she told me. That's good news for the many guests of the "Taj Mahal". "My parents taught me to cook," says Bina. "And then I learned much more about food at college. Of course, we offer fish and chips at the restaurant too. But most people who come to us want Indian food." Now, where would we be without people like Bina and her Indian food? – Hungry!

Timo Roth is an electrician from Germany. He puts solar panels on English houses for a German company. "I travel all over England in the week," Timo says. "But I love the weekends here. We all go out together." Timo has got many friends here. At the rugby club, for example. "It said 'Rugby Football Club' at the door," he told me. "So I went in and asked if I could play football. I was quite surprised when I saw the shape of the ball! But now I love the game." And our town loves you, Timo. You're our star player!

Another German, **Nadja Jung**, works as a baker at Dobbs Bakery. Jim Dobbs told me why he wanted a German baker. "Well, German bakers get fantastic training. And everybody loves German bread and cakes. So I found Nadja and together we made this new bread that we call 'Wunderbread'." Then I spoke to Nadja. "I love it here. The people are really nice and polite. I'm making a lot of 'Wunderbread' at the moment, but I'm going to learn how to make English things too. Most Germans don't like English bread, but I love toast and marmalade and a cup of tea in the mornings. Very English – and very good!" Yes, just like you, Nadja. Wunderbar!

Piotr Szwarc is a plumber from Poland. He likes it here, but he gets angry sometimes. "People in England make jokes about us," he says. "They say that we don't speak English, don't work hard and take away jobs from English people." Unfortunately, Piotr is right. Yes, that IS what some English people think ... Piotr says, "Listen to me. I speak good English. And I work very hard. And just look around you – there's enough work here for everybody." I know Piotr is right, because I couldn't find a plumber to repair my shower. That has been done now – Piotr is quick! We need people like you, Piotr. Please stay!

Vocabulary: Ich bin ... / Etwas ist ...

I'm ... angry, awake, crazy, enthusiastic, excited, glad, hungry, interested, pleased, surprised.
Something is ... allowed, attached, classy, clear, different, fast, furnished, hard, idiotic, meaningful, necessary, real, required, short, special, thin, unusual, used.

immigrant Immigrant/in, Einwanderer/in
to notice bemerken
different anders; andere/r/s
Indian indisch
chips Pommes frites
electrician Elektriker/in
solar panel Sonnenkollektor
shape Form
another ein/e andere/r/s
baker Bäcker/in
marmalade Marmelade aus Zitrusfrüchten
plumber Installateur/in, Anlagenmechaniker/in für Sanitär-, Heizungs- und Klimatechnik
Poland Polen
hard hart
enough genug
shower Dusche

A **Match the names A – D to the photos 1 – 6. Two photos do not match.**
Ordnen Sie die Namen A – D den Fotos 1 – 6 zu. Zwei Fotos passen zu keinem Namen.

A Bina **B** Nadja **C** Piotr **D** Timo

1

2

3

4

5

6

B **Who's talking? Choose the right person for sentences 1 – 5.**
Wer spricht? Wählen Sie die richtige Person für die Sätze 1 – 5.

Bina • Nadja • Piotr • Rebecca • Timo

1 "I work all the time, so I really don't have time for hobbies." ____________
2 "I'm so glad that I know a good plumber now." ____________
3 "When my parents came to visit me here, they brought their own bread!" ____________
4 "I love going out to the pub with my friends after a game." ____________
5 "Our most popular meal is 'Chicken Tikka Masala', of course." ____________

C **EXAM** **Find the right word in the text for definitions 1 – 5.**
Finden Sie zu den Worterklärungen 1 – 5 das passende Wort im Text.

1 see or hear somebody or something: ____________
2 a person who is staying at a hotel, eating at a restaurant, etc.: ____________
3 go from one place to another: ____________
4 very, very good: ____________
5 something that you say or do to make people laugh: ____________

D **Rebecca's plans. Finish the sentences with the right going to-form.**
Rebeccas Pläne. Vervollständigen Sie die Sätze mit der richtigen *going to*-Form.

1 My boyfriend and I ____________ [**live**] in the USA.
2 He ____________ [**look**] for a job there soon.
3 He's a chef so it ____________ [**not be**] difficult for him.
4 But before that, I ____________ [**write**] a few more newspaper articles and earn some money!

Ziel: Ich kann einem Text die wichtigsten Informationen entnehmen.

A1.20

Tip: You don't have to understand every word.

In England

If you come to England, you'll find that most English people are very tolerant. But it's only polite to try and adjust to the customs of your guest country. And it's easy! The most important thing is to be polite. Always. Just say "please", "thank you" and "sorry" as often as possible. It will make things a lot easier for you.

Being polite is the reason for another important custom, queuing. In England, more than two people will always form an orderly queue. Join them – at the end, of course! And now that you're waiting in the queue, you could try and talk to the person standing next to you.

All English people love small talk! It's very important to start any conversation with some sentences about the weather, the traffic, TV or sports. If you know the person you are talking to, use their first name.

This is also very English, by the way: Everybody calls each other by their first name instead of Mr/Ms So-and-so. Most of the time, employees even call their boss by his or her first name! That does not necessarily mean that they're good friends.

And finally another important English custom that you'll perhaps like more than the other ones: the After-Work-Drink. Colleagues go to the pub after work to have a drink together. Sounds great, doesn't it? And it's fun! But you have to know that people buy each other "rounds" (instead of paying for their individual drinks) at the bar. No server will come to serve your pints of beer or glasses of wine. You go to the bar, ask for the drinks, pay for them and take them back to your colleagues' table. Easy, really – and very polite!

to adjust (sich) anpassen
custom Sitte, Brauch, Gewohnheit
possible möglich
queuing; queue Schlange stehen; (Warte-)Schlange
to form bilden
to join (sich) anschließen
small talk Geplauder
traffic Verkehr
first name Vorname
to buy a round eine Runde ausgeben
pint „Halbe" (0,568 Liter)
to warn warnen
to shake hands Hände schütteln, sich die Hand geben

A What is the text about in general? Tick the best summary.
Wovon handelt der Text ganz allgemein? Machen Sie ein Häkchen an die beste Zusammenfassung.

A ☐ The text warns you about the mistakes that tourists to England often make.
B ☐ The text is about the rules of conversation in England.
C ☐ The text talks about English customs that visitors to England should know about.
D ☐ The text is about what to do in an English pub.

B Tick the five important customs that the text talks about.
Machen Sie ein Häkchen an die fünf wichtigen Gewohnheiten, die im Text erwähnt werden.

1 ☐ being open
2 ☐ buying rounds
3 ☐ shaking hands
4 ☐ using first names
5 ☐ looking smart
6 ☐ queuing
7 ☐ making jokes
8 ☐ using small talk
9 ☐ playing sports
10 ☐ being polite

C Choose exercise 1, 2 or 3.
Wählen Sie Aufgabe 1, 2 oder 3.

1 Explain three of the customs in German.
Erklären Sie drei der Gewohnheiten auf Deutsch.

2 Explain two of the customs in English.
Erklären Sie zwei der Gewohnheiten auf Englisch.

3 Think of a German custom and write it down in English.
Überlegen Sie sich eine deutsche Sitte und schreiben Sie sie in Englisch auf.

Ziel: Ich kann vom Englischen ins Deutsche vermitteln.

D **Finish the German sentences.**
Vervollständigen Sie die deutschen Sätze.

Sie machen eine Ausbildung bei einem Maschinenhersteller. Ein japanischer Kunde Ihrer Firma schickt einen Notruf, dort ist eine wichtige Maschine ausgefallen. Zusammen mit zwei Kollegen sollen Sie nach Japan reisen, um die Maschine zu reparieren.

Sie fragen Ihre englische Freundin, die einige Zeit in Japan gelebt hat, per Mail, was die wichtigsten Regeln sind, die man in Japan beachten muss, und erhalten eine ausführliche Antwort.

Schicken Sie die Mail an Ihre Kollegen weiter und fassen Sie dabei die wichtigsten Regeln knapp auf Deutsch zusammen.

1 I was really quite surprised at how extremely polite Japanese people are. Politeness is even more important than in England! You just cannot be too polite in Japan.

Das Wichtigste ist: Seid immer ______________________________.

2 Even though business people know that Europeans normally shake hands when they meet, shaking hands isn't usually done in Japan. People – men and women – bow instead.
Be careful not to hit the other person's head, though!

Gebt Japanern nicht die Hand zur Begrüßung, sondern ______________________________.

3 Don't wear socks that have got holes in them because if you're invited to somebody's home, you'll have to take off your shoes and leave them in the front area before you go in.

Wenn ihr bei jemandem zu Hause eingeladen seid, müsst ihr beim Eintreten

______________________________.

4 The Japanese love presents – well, who doesn't? Always take a present when you're invited to somebody's home. It shouldn't be expensive, though.

Wenn ihr bei jemandem zu Hause eingeladen seid, solltet ihr ______________________________

______________________________.

5 Now this one is interesting as well: I don't know why, but if you give or receive something (no matter if it's a present or simply a business card), always use both your hands!

Wenn ihr etwas überreicht oder in Empfang nehmt, benutzt immer ______________________________.

6 You should never eat or drink while you're walking down the street. It's impolite to do so in Japan. If you're really hungry or thirsty, just get yourself something from a vending machine and stand next to the machine to eat or drink it.

In Japan gilt es als unhöflich, im Gehen etwas ______________________________

______________________________.

Grammar: Über Tätigkeiten sprechen → G15

Shaking hands is a German custom.
Das Händeschütteln ist ein deutscher Brauch.

Being polite is important in England.
In England ist es wichtig, höflich zu sein.

to bow
sich verbeugen

to hit
stoßen, treffen

hole
Loch

to take off
ausziehen

business card
Visitenkarte

Grammar Check 1: *Going to-future (I'm going to find a new job.)*

Kreuzen Sie die richtige Antwort an. Tragen Sie den Lösungsbuchstaben (nach dem Pfeil) unten auf der Seite ein.

1 Ich benutze das *going to-future*, um zu sagen, was ich

A ☐ mag. → E
B ☐ vorhabe. → A
C ☐ kann. → I

2 Ich bilde das *going to-future*, indem ich **vor** dem *going to* eine Form von

A ☐ be → B
B ☐ do → D
C ☐ have → L

benutze.

3 Hinter dem *going to* benutze ich

A ☐ ein Verb in der Grundform. → R
B ☐ ein Nomen. → S
C ☐ eine Zeitangabe. → W

Carol is going to ride her bike all day.

Grammar Check 2: Bedingungssätze

Kreuzen Sie die richtige Antwort an. Tragen Sie den Lösungsbuchstaben (nach dem Pfeil) unten auf der Seite ein.

4 Wenn ich eine Bedingung nennen will, benutze ich

A ☐ when → E
B ☐ of → I
C ☐ if → O

If I've got enough money, I'll buy another round.

5 In Bedingungssätzen benutze ich in den beiden Satzteilen

A ☐ nur die Grundform. → O
B ☐ zweimal dieselbe Zeitform. → E
C ☐ zwei verschiedene Zeitformen. → A

6 In dem Satzteil ohne *if* benutze ich

A ☐ das going to-future. → M
B ☐ das will-future. → D
C ☐ die Grundform. → T

Tragen Sie die Lösungsbuchstaben hier ein. Sind alle Fragen richtig gelöst, ergibt sich ein Wort aus dieser Unit.

5	2	3	4	1	6

Vocabulary Check 1: Ein Wort passt nicht

Kreuzen Sie das Wort an, das **nicht** in den Satz passt. Tragen Sie den Lösungbuchstaben (nach dem Pfeil) weiter unten ein.

1 I'm going to work as a

A ☐ baker. → S
B ☐ plumber. → T
C ☐ guest. → R
D ☐ tour guide. → N

2 I'm going to go to

A ☐ Swedish. → W
B ☐ England. → B
C ☐ Italy. → C
D ☐ Spain. → L

3 I'd like some

A ☐ chips → E
B ☐ toast → U
C ☐ marmalade → I
D ☐ traffic → A

with my meal.

4 In England people

A ☐ form → T
B ☐ buy → N
C ☐ wait in → D
D ☐ join → S queues.

Lösungswort:

2	3	1	4

Vocabulary Check 2: Kreuzworträtsel

Tragen Sie die englischen Begriffe für die Wörter rechts in das Kreuzworträtsel ein.

Waagerecht →
2 Elektriker/in
4 Sitte, Gewohnheit
5 anpassen
9 Loch
10 vorbei
11 genug
12 Bauarbeiter/in
13 treffen
14 Weile

Senkrecht ↓
1 hart
2 aufgeregt
3 bemerken
6 bilden
7 Dusche
8 durch
12 (sich) verbeugen

Video lounge

V7 BBC Motion Gallery

The wannabe

Pick the right word and complete the sentences.
Wählen Sie das richtige Wort und vervollständigen Sie die Sätze.

audition • modelling agency • plastic surgery • profile • talent

1 Murat applies to a famous ______________.
2 Murat takes part in an ______________ for young singers, dancers and actors.
3 You need ______________ if you want to become a star.
4 Murat is so worried about his nose that he has ______________.
5 The woman in the agency thinks that Murat has got a beautiful ______________.

A I'm going to do it too!

Complete Tom's sentences with a going to-phrase.

Example: Tim: "My brother worked as a truck driver in the summer."
→ *Tom: "So what? I'm going to work as a truck driver too."*

1 Tim: "My friend Don lived in Sweden for a while."
Tom: "So what? ______________________ in Sweden for a while too."

2 Tim: "He even learned Swedish before he went!"
Tom: "So what? ______________________ Swedish before I go too."

3 Tim: "My colleague Amy asked our boss for more money."
Tom: "So what? ______________________ my boss for more money too."

4 Tim: "Then she went to Italy – on her motorbike!"
Tom: "So what? ______________________ to Italy on a motorbike too."

5 Tim: "Unfortunately she had a terrible accident there."
Tom: "So what? ______________________ a terrible accident too – what?? No, I'm not!!"

B In the lunch break

Circle the right form. (Look at the Grammar box on page 79 for help.)

1 "If the boss [agrees] [will agree], we'll watch the match together."

2 "Listen, if United win this match, [I] [I'll] buy the first round in the pub tonight."

3 "The boss [joins] [will join] us at the pub later if she isn't too tired."

4 "If [you] [you'll] drink too much tonight, you'll have to leave your car here."

5 "If I have to leave the car, [I] [I'll] ask Pete to pick us up."

6 "But I won't go to the pub if United [lose] [will lose] the match!"

C To the pub

Match the questions and the answers. Draw lines.

1 "Where are we going to go after work?"	A "No, he isn't. He's going to go home."
2 "Is Paul going to come with us?"	B "Only if we all agree."
3 "Why aren't Darren and Vicky here?"	C "Well, you're the only one with a bus licence!"
4 "Who's going to drive us all home tonight?"	D "You'll have to have a cola."
5 "Ha, ha. What if I want a drink too?"	E "They're going to come later."
6 "Will you invite the boss?"	F "To the pub, of course."

D Sorry!
EXAM

Fill in the correct English words.

1 English people have ____________________ [ihre] own rules and customs.

2 They are often more polite ____________________ [als] Germans, for example.

3 If you accidentally touch another person, that person will ____________________ [gewöhnlich] say 'sorry'.

4 Of course you ____________________ [sollten] say 'sorry' too!

5 People ____________________ [die] come to England for the first time are often surprised.

6 But you will quickly get used to it – it isn't ____________________ [schwierig].

E Different countries, different customs
Complete the sentences with the verb in the -ing form.
(If you need help, look at the Grammar box on page 83.)

Example:
→ *Making jokes in other countries is always a little dangerous.*

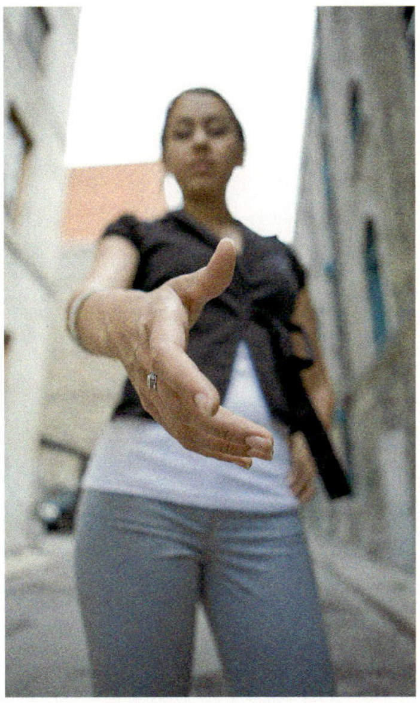

1 ____________________ [find] out about the customs of a country before you go there is important.

2 ____________________ [be] polite means different things in different countries.

3 ____________________ [look] on the internet is the easiest way of getting information.

4 ____________________ [shake] hands is a polite greeting in Germany, for example.

5 But ____________________ [bow] to each other is the custom in Japan.

F I'm going abroad
Schreiben Sie eine Mail an Ihren englischen Freund John und erzählen Sie ihm von Ihren Plänen. Erzählen Sie ihm, dass Sie vorhaben, für ein paar Monate nach Spanien zu gehen und dort in einem Hotel zu arbeiten. Erklären Sie, dass Sie zwar kein Spanisch sprechen, aber man Ihnen gesagt hat, dass Englisch ausreicht. Sagen Sie, dass Sie schon immer für eine Weile ins Ausland gehen wollten, und Sie wirklich aufgeregt sind.
Wenn Sie Hilfe brauchen, schauen Sie noch einmal Seite 78 an.

Hi John

I'm ____

____

____

____

____

accidentally
versehentlich

greeting
Begrüßung

Textarbeit: Mediation, Statement

A1.27

A new home

Five years ago Maneesha's father came from India to England to work there. When he had saved some money, his family followed him. Maneesha was sixteen then. The first year in England was very hard for her. She did not speak English well and was afraid to go out.

Then an uncle told her about an English course at college and so she started there six months ago. She only goes to college from 9 a.m. to 12.30 p.m. Some days she gets homework but it is never too much. She has long holidays and weekends. She works at a hotel forty hours a week, usually in the evenings or at night, to earn some money. So sometimes Maneesha feels a little tired at college.

Through her English course Maneesha has met people from all over the world – for example from Pakistan, China and Russia. They often compare how people live in different countries. That is very interesting. When she has finished her English course, Maneesha would like to study and find a good job afterwards. (179 words)

Annotations:
line 6 **to be afraid** – Angst haben
line 21 **to compare** – vergleichen

A **Mediation**

Bei einem Vorstellungsgespräch möchte sich die Personalchefin ein Bild von Ihren Englischkenntnissen machen und bittet Sie, ihr das Wichtigste aus dem Text auf Deutsch zusammenzufassen.
Geben Sie den Text oben **sinngemäß auf Deutsch** wieder.
Schreiben Sie bitte einen **zusammenhängenden Text**.
Informieren Sie die Chefin über folgende Punkte:

- Grund für den Umzug von Maneeshas Familie nach England
- Zeitpunkt des Umzugs
- Maneeshas Probleme im ersten Jahr
- Maneeshas Zeiteinteilung für Englischkurs und Arbeit im Hotel
- Arbeitszeiten im Hotel
- das Besondere an Maneeshas Englischkurs
- Maneeshas Zukunftspläne

(If you need help, look at the skills tip on page 40 again.)

B **Statement**

Some people think it is better to leave Germany and live and work in other countries.
Do you think they are right? Why? Why not? Give your opinion.

Write 40 – 50 words in complete English sentences, please.

(If you need help, look at the skills tip on page 52 again.)

Managing Situations: Giving directions

(If you need help, look at the skills tip on page 53 again.)

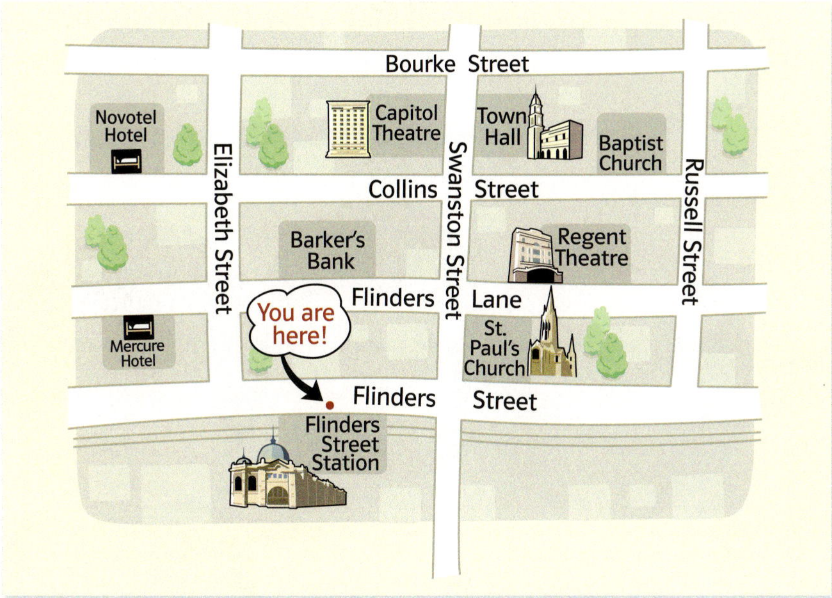

1 You are standing in front of Flinders Street Station.
A tourist asks you: "Can you tell me the way to the Novotel Hotel, please?"
Tell him how to get there.

2 You are standing in front of Flinders Street Station.
A girl asks you: "How can I get to the Baptist Church, please?"
Tell her how to get there.

Vanessa ist Friseurin.
Sie ist froh, dass sie Englisch spricht, denn …

I'm a hairdresser and I work in a great salon at Frankfurt International Airport. Our customers come from all around the world. And what's the most important skill for a hairdresser? That's right – talking! So I often speak English to our customers. I really love my job. It's hard work sometimes because we're usually very busy and we have to stand up all day. But I love it when people leave the salon looking and feeling good. OK, the money could be better, but I often get a good tip from happy clients.

Frisur:
hairstyle
hairdo
haircut

What hairdressers do:
wash • colour • cut • curl •
blow-dry • style

curly hair

straight hair

cornrows

braids

fringe

mohawk

ponytail

Hair colour:
black • blonde • brown •
grey • red
light brown/red/…
dark brown/red/…

Glückliche Friseure!

Hairdressers 'happiest at work'
A new survey found that hairdressers are the happiest workers in the UK, with two out of five saying they are very happy in their job. Why?
We asked them.

Aleesha, 22, says: "Because we make people feel good and look good."

"It's a trendy job. You meet a lot of young people. That's fun," says John, who has been a hairdresser for 14 years.

"Because hairdressers can be their own bosses," says Lisa, who has got her own salon.

"I'm having a bad hair day." That's what people say on a day when they feel ugly and when everything seems to go wrong.

Automaten gibt es überall ...

Things that you can get from machines:

books • bus / train tickets • bread • cigarettes • coffee • drinks • eggs • photos • hot meals • ice cream • lottery tickets • money • newspapers • pizza • wine • shoes • snacks • stamps • toilet paper • umbrellas

What vending machine operatives do:

supply • install •
They fill / clean / service the machines ...
... and they collect the money, of course!

In the 1880s ...

... the first vending machines in England sold postcards.
... the first vending machines in the USA sold chewing gum on station platforms.
... the first vending machines in Germany sold chocolate and other sweets.

NEW

Check out our *digital* vending machines. They offer games, ringtones, logos and pictures for mobile phones.

Sergejs Kunden kommen aus aller Welt. Manchmal spricht er lieber Englisch als Deutsch mit ihnen.

How often do you buy a bottle of cola or some chocolate from a machine? It's something not many people think about: We use machines all the time. My job is to take care of these machines and to make sure they're always full and working. It's a great job. I have to go out to our customers – people who have vending machines in their pub or their snack bar, for example. In Berlin a lot of these people don't speak very good German, and my German isn't that good either. So it's sometimes easier to speak English to them.

Lena arbeitet vorübergehend in Australien.

What's your job?

I work as a retail assistant here in Australia. I sell surfwear and fashion for women.
It's a clothes shop for women but sometimes men come in. It can be really hard explaining to them that they're trying on women's tops!

What are the good points about your job?

I get a great discount on the clothes that I buy for myself! And the hours are flexible.

Any bad points?

It can be a bit annoying when you help someone for about an hour and then they don't buy anything. Also my poor feet hurt from standing up all day.

Would you recommend your job?

Yes. It's great to talk to people all day. And I love the clothes!

A shop assistant typically earns ...
22,404 Canadian dollars in Canada.
23,832 euros in Germany.
£11,688 in the UK.
16,764 euros in Italy.

Do you want to go on a permanent cruise?
Cruise ship is looking for a

Shop Assistant
(Gift Shop Department)

Some retail experience preferred.
Fluent English language required.
Salary range: $1600 – 2000 U.S. per month, depending on commission.

Possibilities for promotion to Assistant Gift Shop Manager.

One of the most important qualities of shop assistants?

Their good mood!

Don't blame me! I'm just the sales assistant!

Wieso hilft es einem Verkäufer, wenn er Englisch kann? Jan erklärt es uns ...

I work in a big department store in Munich. I'm so glad that I can speak some English! There are lots of English and American tourists here. I've learned that they expect you to be super polite – even more so than the Germans. But they're usually very polite themselves, especially the Americans. And when we get tourists from other countries, I can usually speak English to them as well. My English isn't very good, but I make sure that I know the phrases that are important in my job.

Same job, different names:
assistant • shop assistant • sales assistant • salesperson • clerk • sales clerk

Seitdem Lisa einen LKW fährt, spricht sie öfter Englisch. Warum?

I'm a truck driver and I love my job. I always knew that I wanted to become a driver. At first I only drove vans. I delivered parcels. After that I drove my first truck for a local furniture shop. It's not as easy as you think – all those narrow streets! Now I'm a long distance trucker. That was always my dream. It's really cool. And it's good that I can speak a little English because I have to talk to customs' people in other countries. And of course I want to talk to truckers from other countries too.

dustcart

Berufskraftfahrer/innen fahren viele verschiedene Fahrzeuge …

dump truck

delivery truck

So you want to be a dump truck driver in the Australian mining industry? Read this:

Good points:
- You don't have to be very fit.
- You can earn a lot of money.
- It's for men *and* women.

Bad points:
- It's boring work: You drive up and down a big hole all day.
- 12-hour-days are normal.
- You're in the middle of nowhere.

tow truck

bus

Time for a laugh …

A policeman stopped a truck driver and said, "You're the winner of our Safest Driver Contest. Well done! You win £3,000. What are you going to do with the money?"
"Hm, perhaps I should finally get a driving licence", the truck driver answered.

Ohne Englisch geht als Kellner gar nichts, findet Pjeter, denn ...

Here in the Black Forest, lots of guests are tourists from other countries. Not many of them speak German, but most of them speak at least a little English. So if I want to do a good job, I have to give them information and advice in English. Luckily we've got an English language menu in the restaurant. But some people also ask for travel information ("How far is it to ...?") or hiking recommendations ("Where can we go for a long but easy walk?"). And in this job, it's a good idea to be polite and answer the guests' questions: People often give you a bigger tip* if you're friendly!

* **tip** a little extra money that you give to somebody, for example somebody who serves you in a restaurant

A job in a restaurant is all about team work ...

... and it isn't always glamourous.

But if you like people, you'll have fun every day (see below).

The stupidest thing I've ever heard from a guest: "Can you make sure there's no chocolate on my pizza? I'm allergic to chocolate." Chocolate on a pizza?? How do you react to this, if you still want a good tip? Easy – just stay cool and say: "Certainly, Madam. I'll tell the chef*."

* **chef** a cook in a restaurant, hotel, etc.

Did you know?

Nobody gives tips in Japan.

A lot of servers have to wear a kind of smart uniform. Sometimes it's a "dirndl".

Most waiters hate fast food restaurants.

"A photo of Joyce and me in the new restaurant. The food was good, but the service was really slow!"

serve • **service** • **server**

server = **waiter** (male)
waitress (female)

[əd'mɪnɪstrətɪv ə'sɪstənt]
Betonung beachten!

The ideal secretary

Small office is looking for a full-time

Administrative Assistant

You should be
- flexible
- organized
- patient

You should have
- good communication skills
- no problems with numbers
- all the answers!

You will **not** have to
- make coffee
- clean the office rooms
- do overtime!

Find out more on our website:
ww#.officeshare…com

Bürokaufleute haben sogar ihren eigenen Feiertag …

Administrative Professionals' Day (also known as Secretary's Day) is on the Wednesday of the last full week of April. In the United States, the day is often celebrated by giving assistants presents such as flowers, chocolates, lunch at a restaurant, or time off.

What would you choose?

~~"I don't know where me the head stands."~~

AAARGH!

You can't say that in English!
You say:

"I don't know if I'm coming or going."

Christinas Englisch ist jetzt besser – so lange es im Büro nicht zu turbulent wird …

I'm an administrative or admin assistant in a small firm that specializes in building expensive custom-made[1] kitchens. You won't believe how much money some people spend on their kitchen! We even build kitchens for customers in other countries like France and England. I do most of the office work here. I have to deal with phone calls, emails and invoices[2], for example. When customers phone the firm, they usually talk to me first. I took a special English course (my boss paid for it) so I can explain things to customers, especially money things. I've become quite good at it – except sometimes it's so busy here, I forget everything I've learned!

[1] **custom-made** designed and made for one customer
[2] **invoice** a list that shows what the customer must pay

Elena arbeitet in einer Großstadtpraxis und spricht jeden Tag Englisch …

I'm a real 'people person' and my job allows me to deal with new and interesting people from all over the world every day. The best part of my job is seeing that I'm really helping people. Often people are very nervous, because they don't feel well or they're in pain[1] and they're afraid. I learned that if I stay calm[2] and listen to them, I can make them feel better. I'm the best English speaker in this surgery[3], so I can often help. Of course I have to do medical things as well. That's OK with me. I think giving injections and assisting the doctor is more fun than working at the reception.

[1] **to be in pain** Schmerzen haben
[2] **calm** ruhig
[3] **surgery** 1. Praxis, 2. Operation

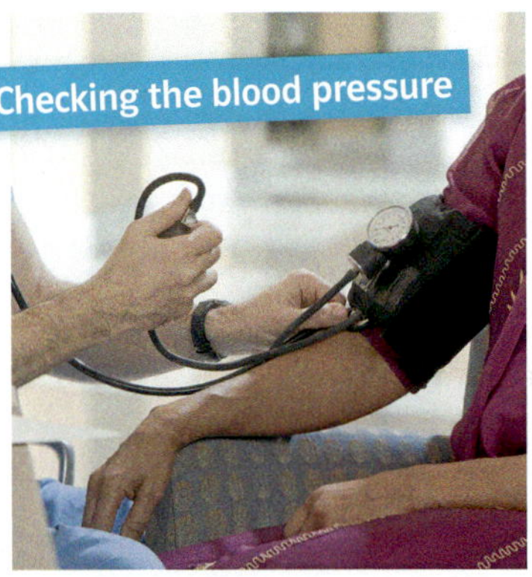
Checking the blood pressure

Giving injections

CLINIC RECEPTIONIST
PRIVATE PRACTICE FOR COSMETIC SURGERY IN LONDON

… The practice does not have a waiting room. The doctor's team of assistants has to make sure that our famous patients will not have to wait.
… We need someone who works well even when the clinic is extremely busy. You have to be a strong team player in our small team. …

Time for a laugh …

In the waiting room of a doctor's surgery
"Oh, hello, Mary. How are you?"
– "Hello, Sandy. I'm fine, thanks."

??? **Fine? Well, what is she doing in a doctor's surgery then?**

Different doctors:
general practitioner (GP)
paediatrician (children)
ear, nose and throat specialist
orthopaedic specialist
ophthalmologist (eyes)
dermatologist (skin)
dentist (teeth)
vet (animals)

doctor's surgery
doctor's practice
doctor's office
medical practice

Sebastian lebt in Australien und sucht sich seine Aufträge selbst ...

I'm a qualified painter and decorator, trained and educated in Germany.
My services include: exterior and interior work on private houses, renovations to private/commercial buildings.
I am experienced, professional and my work is 100% customer-orientated.
I have my own tools[1] and van.
Please give me a call and ask for a quote[2]:
040556225 (Sebastian)

[1]| **tools** Werkzeuge
[2]| **quote** Angebot, Kostenvoranschlag

Some typical painting and decorating jobs:

- taking off old wallpaper and hanging new paper
- preparing wood, plaster, metal or other surfaces* for painting
- restoring old interior or exterior decor
- protecting surfaces from dirt and damp

*| **surface** Oberfläche

Colours have the funniest names. Everybody knows **red**, **yellow** and **blue**.
You might even have heard of **magenta**.
But did you know **cayenne** or **ice**? And what name would you give **this colour**?

Kerim lernt wieder Englisch, denn er hat einen Plan ...

I love being a painter and decorator, because the work is never boring. I work indoors and outdoors. I work on a building site[1], around a house or in the firm's workshop. Often I'm part of a team, but sometimes I don't see a colleague all day. Of course I have to use paintbrushes[2], but I have to deal with lots of different machines too. And I love the moment when the work is done. Everything looks nice and fresh and clean – and the customers are very happy! I'm learning English again at the moment because I want to go abroad for a while. Workers with my skills are wanted almost anywhere in the world.

[1]| **building site** Baustelle
[2]| **paintbrush** Pinsel

Mobiles

to **turn on**	einschalten, anmachen	↔ to turn off *(ausschalten)*
to **answer the phone**	ans Telefon gehen	↔ to phone/call/ring somebody *(jemanden anrufen)*
to **receive**	erhalten	↔ to send *(senden)*
to **text**	eine SMS-Nachricht verschicken, „simsen"	= to send a text
phone	Telefon	
mobile (phone)	Handy	! not "handy"
headphones	Kopfhörer	! a pair of headphones
earphones	Ohrhörer	! a pair of earphones
ringtone	Klingelton	→ to ring
text	SMS	→ to text

At the hairdresser's

hairdresser	Friseur/in	→ hair
customer	Kunde/Kundin	
appointment	Termin, Verabredung	to make an appointment
coat	Mantel, Jacke	to wear a coat
to **curl**	kräuseln, aufdrehen	→ curly *(lockig)*
to **dry**	trocknen	→ dry *(trocken)*

Emails

subject	Betreff	
meaningful	aussagekräftig	→ to mean *(bedeuten)*
clear	klar, deutlich	
Yours sincerely	Mit freundlichen Grüßen	
rule	Regel, Vorschrift	to follow a rule *(eine Regel befolgen)*
allowed	erlaubt	→ to allow *(erlauben)*
to **avoid**	vermeiden	
joke	Witz	→ to joke *(einen Witz machen, scherzen)*

Internet forms

to **register (with)**	sich anmelden (bei)	
to **enter**	eingeben	↔ to delete *(löschen)*
to **select**	auswählen	= to pick
to **tick**	ankreuzen, abhaken	
title	Anrede	
details	(Adress-)Daten, Angaben	
company	Firma	= firm
advertising	Werbung	→ advert *(Anzeige)*
field	Feld	

Phrases

phrase	Redewendung, Ausdruck
Certainly.	Sicher. Selbstverständlich.
Go on.	Nur zu. Mach(en Sie) schon.
Well done!	Gut gemacht!

Time phrases

all the time	die ganze Zeit	I listen to music all the time.
almost	beinahe, fast	Your hair is almost ready to dry.
already	schon, bereits	

Symbole: = Synonym; ↔ Gegensatz; → Wortfamilie; ! Achtung

A **Odd one out. Which word does not belong in the group? Underline it.**
Welches Wort gehört nicht in die Gruppe? Unterstreichen Sie das Wort.

1 word • phrase • phone • sentence
2 break • enter • select • tick
3 receive • send • text • clean
4 cut • cry • curl • dry

B **Pick the right phrase and write three answers.**
Wählen Sie den richtigen Ausdruck und schreiben Sie drei Antworten.

Certainly. • Go on. • Good morning. • Well done!

1 I've passed my test. – ____________________
2 Can I have a cup of tea, please? – ____________________
3 Oh. My phone is ringing. Can I answer it? – ____________________

C **What's the word? Complete the words with the letters on the left.**
Wie heißt das Wort? Vervollständigen Sie die Wörter mit den Buchstaben links.

1 CUTJEB s____________________
2 ENTSVIDRI a____________________g
3 DRYALE a____________________
4 FAIENGUN m____________________l
5 SREAH p____________________
6 LOWLE a____________________d

D **Pick the right word in sentences 1–4 and circle it.**
Wählen Sie das passende Wort in den Sätzen 1–4 und umkringeln Sie es.

1 Listen. I've got a new ringtone on my headphones / mobile phone.
2 The company / customer doesn't have an appointment.
3 Avoid jokes / rules in formal emails.
4 Tick this box if you want to receive / register our newsletter.

E **Complete the sentences with the right word or words.**
Vervollständigen Sie die Sätze mit dem passenden Wort / den passenden Wörtern.

1 A ____________________ is a person who helps people look good.
2 You put "____________________" at the end of an email.
3 The ____________________ was good when everybody laughs.
4 In an internet form, you have to ____________________ your details.
5 If you want to listen to the radio, you have to ____________ it ____________ first.
6 You wear a ____________________ in cold or rainy weather.

Friends

gender	Geschlecht	
male	männlich	↔ female
female	weiblich	↔ male
to **make friends**	Freundschaften schließen	→ to be friends *(befreundet sein)*
friendship	Freundschaft	→ friend
relationship	Beziehung	
boyfriend	(fester) Freund	↔ girlfriend
girlfriend	(feste) Freundin	↔ boyfriend
partner	Partner/in	
classmate	Klassenkamerad/in	→ class *(Klasse)*
interested in	interessiert an	→ interest *(Interesse)*; interesting *(interessant)*
looking for	auf der Suche nach	→ to look for *(suchen)*
in touch	in Verbindung	Let's keep in touch.
to **share**	teilen	
to **understand**	verstehen	
feeling	Gefühl	→ to feel *(fühlen)*
thought	Gedanke	→ to think *(denken)*
both	beide	

Internet

site, website	Webseite	
social network	soziales Netzwerk	Do you use social networks?
community	Gemeinschaft	
profile	Profil, Selbstdarstellung	
wall	(Pinn-)Wand	
membership	Mitgliedschaft	→ member *(Mitglied)*
basic info	allgemeine Informationen	→ information
status	Status	
current location	derzeitiger Wohnort	
political views	politische Einstellung	
favourite	Lieblings-	
to **blog**	bloggen	→ blog
to **chat**	chatten	→ chat
to **download**	downloaden, herunterladen	to download a song from the internet
to **email/mail**	mailen	→ email/mail
to **post something**	etwas ins Internet stellen	
to **skype**	skypen	

Work

firm	Firma	= company, business
production	Produktion	→ to produce *(herstellen)*
canteen	Kantine	We have our lunch in the canteen.
lunch break	Mittagspause	→ lunch *(Mittagessen)*
job interview	Vorstellungsgespräch	to be invited for a job interview *(zu einem Vorstellungsgespräch eingeladen sein)*
boss	Chef/in	
colleague	Kollege, Kollegin	
customer	Kunde, Kundin	Always be polite to our customers!
junior reporter	Nachwuchsreporter/in	
machine operator	Maschinenführer/in	Alex works as a machine operator.
management assistant	Bürokauffrau/-mann	

Something is ...

classy	edel, elegant	a classy restaurant
crazy	verrückt	Are you crazy?
idiotic	idiotisch	an idiotic idea

Phrases

all over the world	überall auf der Welt	
by the way	übrigens	
Go ahead.	Mach nur./Machen Sie nur.	

Symbole: = Synonym; ↔ Gegensatz; → Wortfamilie; ! Achtung

A **Pick the right word ending (on the right) for each beginning (1–11) and write the words in your exercise book.**
Suchen Sie das richtige Wortende (rechts) für jeden Wortanfang (1–11) und schreiben Sie die Wörter in Ihr Heft.

1 boy…
2 class…
3 friend…
4 girl…
5 inter…
6 loca…
7 member…
8 net…
9 produc…
10 relation…
11 web…

friend | mate | ship | site | tion | view | work

B **Put in the English words for the German words.**
Tragen Sie die englischen Wörter für die deutschen Wörter (neben dem Rätsel) ein.

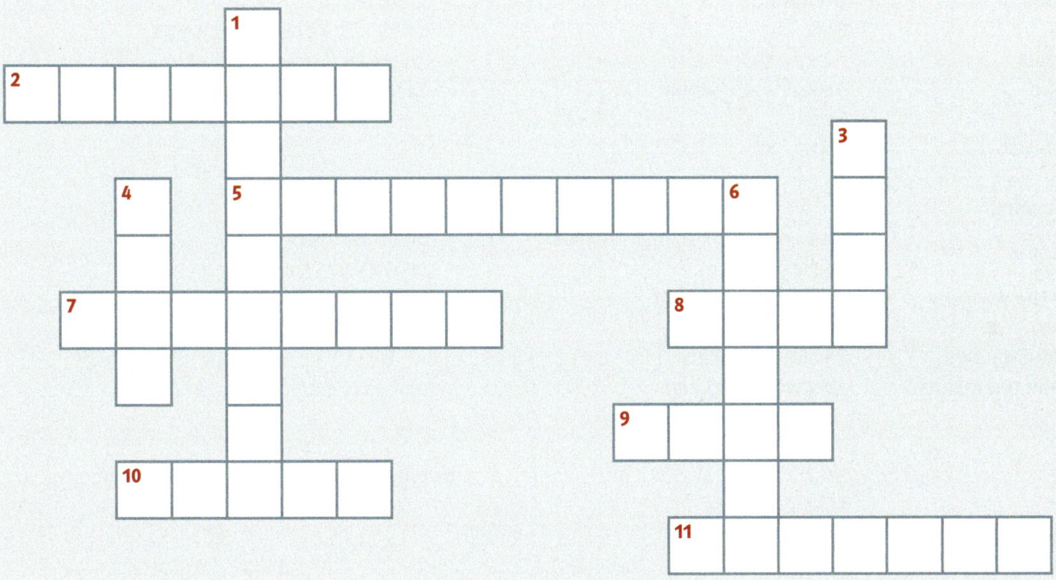

Waagerecht →
2 Netzwerk
5 Mitgliedschaft
7 downloaden
8 ins Internet stellen
9 mailen
10 skypen
11 Webseite

Senkrecht ↓
1 Gemeinschaft
3 chatten
4 bloggen
6 Profil, Selbstdarstellung

C **Complete the sentences with the right word from the word list "Work" on the left page.**
Vervollständigen Sie die Sätze mit dem richtigen Wort aus der Wortliste zu „Work" auf der linken Seite.

1 I work for a big ____________________. They make windows.
2 I'm a management assistant. I often have to talk to our ____________________s. It's fun.
3 I really like my ____________________s. Most of them are my friends too.
4 We often go out after work. Sometimes our ____________________ comes with us!
5 Sandra and I usually have our __________ __________ together. But we don't go in the canteen.
6 But Sandra hopes that she can find a new job. Her first ______ __________ is next week.

Unit 3 – A place of my own

Looking for a flat

flat	Wohnung	= apartment
flat hunting	Wohnungssuche	→ to hunt *(jagen)*
a place of my own	meine eigene Bleibe	
to **move out**	ausziehen	→ to move *(umziehen)*
upstairs	oben (im Haus)	↔ downstairs
downstairs	unten (im Haus)	↔ upstairs
floor	Etage, Stockwerk	on the first floor *(in der ersten Etage)*
size	Größe	
neighbour	Nachbar/in	
advert	Anzeige	→ advertising *(Werbung)*

In the flat

furnished	möbliert	→ to furnish *(möblieren)*
furniture	Möbel	→ furnished
bed	Bett	→ bedroom *(Schlafzimmer)*
chair	Stuhl	
cupboard	Schrank	
shelf, shelves	Regal, Regale	
table	Tisch	= desk
oven	Backofen	Ben is taking the cookies out of the oven.
cable TV	Kabelfernsehen	
broadband	Breitband	
wood	Holz	This table is made out of wood.
to **repair**	reparieren	↔ to break *(kaputt machen)*
to **paint**	malen, anstreichen	→ painter *(Maler/in, Anstreicher/in)*
paint	Farbe	
paintbrush	Farbpinsel	

Housework

to **clean**	saubermachen, reinigen, putzen	→ clean *(sauber)*
to **cook**	kochen	→ cook *(Koch/Köchin)*
to **do the washing**	die Wäsche machen	
to **iron**	bügeln	→ iron *(Bügeleisen)*
to **make the bed**	das Bett machen	
to **wash the dishes**	abwaschen, spülen	→ dishes *(Geschirr)*

Food

salad	Salat	tomato salad
carrot	Möhre, Karotte	
cookies	Kekse	

Something is ...

awful	furchtbar	= terrible
interesting	interessant	↔ boring
unusual	ungewöhnlich	→ usually

Phrases

What would you like?	Was wünschen Sie?
I'd like ...	Ich hätte gern ...
Anything else?	Noch etwas?
Here you are.	Hier, bitte.
Too bad.	Schade.

Time phrases

right now	im Augenblick	= at the moment
just	gerade, soeben	

Symbole: = Synonym; ↔ Gegensatz; → Wortfamilie; ! Achtung

A **Find 10 words. They are all things in a flat.**
Finden Sie 10 Wörter. Es sind alles Dinge in einer Wohnung.

F	R	O	P	S	E	C	Y	L	A	N	T	I	D	E	R
L	O	U	N	K	E	M	T	W	Z	Y	N	O	P	R	A
A	S	B	O	P	N	G	E	I	S	K	E	F	T	V	W
J	E	E	N	T	O	G	S	N	R	S	O	F	A	P	L
E	C	U	P	B	O	A	R	D	A	H	O	U	B	X	P
P	H	I	L	T	E	D	M	O	V	E	N	Z	L	U	C
K	A	N	D	E	Y	P	L	W	G	L	A	B	E	D	W
Y	I	N	T	R	I	K	T	E	R	F	R	O	P	O	H
G	R	A	U	N	S	K	Y	T	R	A	W	L	M	O	N
B	E	S	G	I	N	T	F	U	R	N	I	T	U	R	E
P	R	E	A	N	W	R	I	G	H	B	O	V	R	D	S

B **What housework are these people doing? Look at the photos and complete sentences 1–6.**
Welche Hausarbeit machen diese Menschen? Schauen Sie sich die Fotos an und vervollständigen Sie die Sätze 1–6.

1

2

3

4
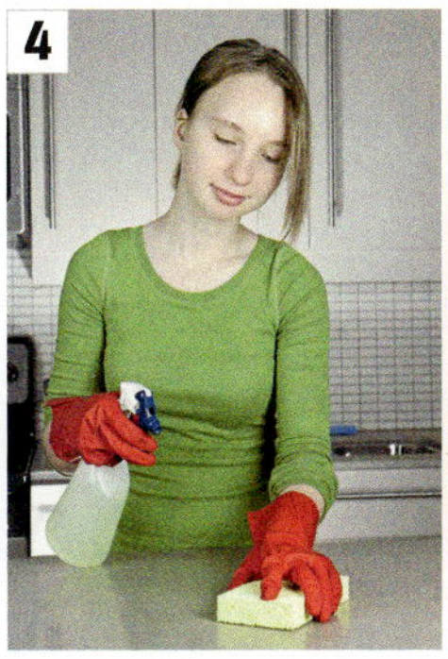
5

6

1 Jamie is ironing.
2 Maria is doing the washing.
3 Tim is cooking.
4 Cassie is cleaning up the kitchen.
5 Irina is making the bed.
6 Pedro is washing the dishes.

C **Complete the questions.**
Vervollständigen Sie die Fragen.

1 Wie fragen Sie, ob Ihre Freundin Hilfe bei der Wohnungssuche braucht?
"Do you need help with your ______________________?"

2 Was sagen Sie, wenn Sie wissen wollen, auf welchem Stockwerk die Wohnung ist?
"On which ______________________ is the flat?"

3 Was sagen Sie, wenn Sie fragen wollen, ob das Badezimmer oben oder unten im Haus ist?
"Is the bathroom ______________________ or ______________________?"

Moving

on the move	in Bewegung	→ to move *(sich bewegen)*
driving lessons	Fahrstunden	
driving licence	Führerschein	
driving test	Führerscheinprüfung	to pass the driving test *(die Führerscheinprüfung bestehen)*
to **pass**	bestehen	↔ to fail *(durchfallen)*
public transport	öffentlicher Nahverkehr	
flight	Flug	→ to fly
hiking trip	Wandertour	→ to hike *(wandern)*
accident	Unfall	
to **drive**	*(selbst)* fahren	→ (bus/car/train) driver
to **fly**	fliegen	→ flight
to **cycle**, to **ride**	Rad fahren	→ cycling *(Radfahren)*
to **walk**	gehen	= to go on foot
to **rent**	mieten	→ rent *(Miete)*
to **pick somebody up**	jemanden abholen	
to **get (to ...)**	(nach ...) kommen, gelangen	
to **change trains**	umsteigen	
to **get off**	aussteigen	↔ to get in (the car), to get on (the bus, the train) *(einsteigen)*
to **crash the car into something**	mit dem Auto in etwas hineinkrachen	→ car crash *(Autounfall)*

Cars etc.

motorbike	Motorrad	to ride a motorbike
camper van	Wohnmobil	
lorry, truck	LKW	→ trucker *(LKW-Fahrer/in)*
van	(Klein-)Transporter	
wreck	Wrack	
satnav	Satellitennavigationssystem, „Navi"	
(car) boot	Kofferraum	
used	gebraucht	↔ new

Giving directions

directions	Wegbeschreibung	to give somebody directions to something *(jemandem den Weg zu etwas beschreiben)*
advice	Ratschlag	to give advice *(einen Rat geben)*
you should	du solltest	
mustn't	nicht dürfen	
to **follow**	folgen, befolgen	to follow advice *(einen Rat befolgen)*
to **cross**	überqueren	to cross a street *(eine Straße überqueren)*
to **turn left/right**	links/rechts abbiegen	→ to turn around *(sich umdrehen)*
along	entlang	
around	in der Nähe	
between	zwischen	
in front of	vor	↔ behind
next to	neben	
opposite	gegenüber (von)	
right through	direkt durch	
straight ahead	geradeaus	Go straight ahead.
to **be lost**	sich verlaufen/verirrt haben	We are lost. We need directions.

In town

church	Kirche	
department store	Kaufhaus	She works in a department store.
pub	Kneipe	
phone box	Telefonzelle	

Time phrases

after that	danach	↔ before that
in time	rechtzeitig, pünktlich	↔ to be early/late *(zu früh/spät dran sein)*

Symbole: = Synonym; ↔ Gegensatz; → Wortfamilie; **!** Achtung

A **Whose are they? Match the owners (1–5) with the vehicles and complete the sentences.**
Wem gehören sie? Ordnen Sie den Besitzern/Besitzerinnen (1–5) die Fahrzeuge zu und vervollständigen Sie die Sätze.

1

Ricky

2

Linda

3

Louis and Kim

4

Paula

5

Andrew

A

B

C

D

E

1 ☐ Ricky drives the ____________________. It's his job.
2 ☐ Linda rides her ____________________ in her free time.
3 ☐ Louis and Kim go on holiday in their ____________________.
4 ☐ Paula is tired. She drives her ____________________ all day.
5 ☐ Andrew often goes for long trips on his ____________________.

B **Complete the words with the right letter.**
Vervollständigen Sie die Wörter mit dem jeweils richtigen Buchstaben.

1 adv __ ce, fl __ ght, d __ rect __ ons
2 b __ __ t, f __ ll __ w, __ pp __ site
3 aro __ nd, ch __ rch, p __ b
4 b __ tw __ __ n, cycl __, wr __ ck
5 __ ccident, __ long, s __ tn __ v

C **What do these words mean? Tick the right answer.**
Was bedeuten diese Wörter? Machen Sie ein Häkchen an die richtige Antwort.

1 public transport:
- A ☐ buses and trains which people use to travel
- B ☐ a very long bus for many people
- C ☐ lorries that everybody can use

2 department store:
- A ☐ a small shop in a small town
- B ☐ a big shop that sells many different things
- C ☐ a shop that only sells very cheap things

3 to pick somebody up:
- A ☐ to go in your car and get somebody who is waiting for you
- B ☐ to stop and talk to somebody
- C ☐ to help somebody who had an accident

Applying for a job

advertised	ausgeschrieben	→ advert *(Anzeige)*; to advertise *(werben)*
to **apply (for)**	sich bewerben (um)	→ application
application	Bewerbung	→ to apply
apprenticeship	Lehre, Ausbildung	to do an apprenticeship *(eine Ausbildung machen)*
position	(Arbeits-)Stelle	= job
requirement	Anforderung	
qualification	Qualifikation; Voraussetzung	
training	Schulung, Einarbeitung	→ to train *(schulen, ausbilden; trainieren)*
skill	Fähigkeit, Fertigkeit	→ skilled *(ausgebildet, qualifiziert)*
experience	Erfahrung	→ experienced *(erfahren)*
CV	Lebenslauf	
job interview	Vorstellungsgespräch	to invite someone to a job interview *(jemanden zum Vorstellungsgespräch einladen)*
opportunity	Möglichkeit, Gelegenheit	
enthusiastic	engagiert	
to **be a team player**	teamfähig sein	
to **be able**	in der Lage sein	= can
to **recommend**	empfehlen	
attached	beigefügt, angehängt	→ to attach *(beifügen, anhängen)*

Jobs

(shop) assistant	Verkäufer/in	to work as a shop assistant
car mechanic	Automechaniker/in	
chauffeur	Chauffeur/in, Fahrer/in	
personal assistant	persönliche/r Assistent/in	
salesperson	Verkaufsangestellte/r	→ to sell *(verkaufen)*
singer	Sänger/in	→ to sing *(singen)*
tour guide	Reiseleiter/in	

Language skills

language	Sprache	
native speaker	Muttersprachler/in	→ to speak *(sprechen)*
fluently	fließend	
to **sound**	sich anhören	→ sound *(Klang)*

Clothes

look	Aussehen	→ to look
suit	Anzug; Kostüm	to wear a suit *(einen Anzug tragen)*
blouse	Bluse	
skirt	Rock	
shirt	Hemd	
tie	Krawatte	
leather shoes	Lederschuhe	
coat	Mantel, Jacke	
smart	schick	a smart shirt *(ein schickes Hemd)*
to **wear**	anziehen, tragen	
to **suit somebody**	jemandem gut stehen	The shirt suits you.

Phrases

I would	ich würde
if I were you, I'd …	an Ihrer Stelle würde ich …
how to write …	wie man … schreibt
to **look forward to hearing from …**	sich darauf freuen, von … zu hören

Symbole: = Synonym; ↔ Gegensatz; → Wortfamilie; **!** Achtung

A **What are these people wearing? Write the words for the clothes on the lines.**
Was haben diese Menschen an? Schreiben Sie die Wörter für die Kleidungsstücke auf die Linien.

1

2

3

4

5

B **What's my job? Read the statements and guess the job.**
Was ist mein Beruf? Lesen Sie die Aussagen und erraten Sie den Beruf.

1. I take groups of people around. I show them interesting places. I talk a lot. I answer questions.

   I'm a ______________________.

2. I know a lot about cars. If there's a problem with a car, I usually find it. Then I repair the car.

   I'm a ______________________.

3. I talk to customers. I show them the things that they are interested in. I give them advice.

   I'm a ______________________.

4. I work for a hotel. I drive people around. I help them with their bags. I have to wear special clothes.

   I'm a ______________________.

5. I work for a famous person. I help her organize her life. I answer her mails. I make her appointments.

   I'm a ______________________.

6. I have to travel a lot. I'm part of a group. I don't always have work. I love my job because I love music.

   I'm a ______________________.

C **Complete the sentences with the right word.**
Vervollständigen Sie die Sätze mit dem richtigen Wort.

application • enthusiastic • languages • qualifications • suits

1. The job advert sounds really interesting. I'm going to send the firm my ______________________ soon.
2. I'd love to work as a teacher, but I haven't got the ______________________.
3. My friend loves his job with the children. He's so ______________________, he only talks about the job now.
4. You speak three ______________________ fluently – it's going to be easy for you to find a job as a tour guide.
5. The suit that you're going to wear for the job interview ______________________ you a lot.

Talking

conversation	Gespräch	= talk, dialogue
to **discuss**	diskutieren	→ discussion
to **agree**	zustimmen	↔ to disagree *(anderer Meinung sein)*
to **complain**	sich beschweren	→ complaint *(Beschwerde)*
to **mind**	etwas dagegen haben	
to **decide**	(sich) entscheiden	→ decision *(Entscheidung)*
to **ask somebody**	jemanden bitten	
to **present**	vorstellen, präsentieren	→ presentation *(Vorstellung)*
to **wonder**	sich fragen	
to **promise**	versprechen	→ promise *(Versprechen)*
to **depend**	darauf ankommen	
to **keep your mouth shut**	den Mund halten	
that's why	deshalb	

The world of work

career dream	Berufstraum	
probation	Probezeit	
full-time	Ganztags-	→ half-time *(Halbtags-)*
right	Recht	to be right *(recht haben)*
employee	Angestellte/r	
gardener	Gärtner/in	→ garden
florist	Florist/in	
chef	Koch/Köchin	= cook
to **continue working**	weiter arbeiten	

What people do at work

to **deal with**	sich kümmern um	
to **produce**	herstellen, produzieren	→ production
to **serve**	bedienen; servieren	→ server *(Servierer/in, Kellner/in)*
to **plant**	(ein)pflanzen	→ plant *(Pflanze)*
to **sort**	sortieren	
to **look after**	betreuen	
to **provide**	anbieten	
to **touch**	berühren	
to **draw**	zeichnen	→ drawing *(Zeichnung)*
to **save**	sparen	↔ to spend *(ausgeben)*

Somebody is ...

pleased	zufrieden	
glad	froh	
surprised	überrascht	→ surprise *(Überraschung)*
patient	geduldig	↔ nervous *(nervös)*
serious	ernst	↔ funny *(lustig)*
thin	dünn	↔ fat *(dick)*
welcome	willkommen	

Cars

racing	(Motor-)Rennen	→ racing driver *(Rennfahrer/in)*
Formula One	Formel Eins	
test drive	Probefahrt	
engine	Motor; Maschine	
technical	technisch	
technology	Technologie	→ technical
to **bet**	wetten	→ bet *(Wette)*

Time phrases

before	zuvor, schon einmal	
a few months ago	vor ein paar Monaten	
a waste of time	Zeitverschwendung	

Symbole: = Synonym; ↔ Gegensatz; → Wortfamilie; ! Achtung

A **Pick the right beginning and complete the verbs (1 – 9).**
Wählen Sie den richtigen Wortanfang aus und vervollständigen Sie die Verben (1 – 9).

com • de • dis • pre • pro • won

1 ________mise	4 ________duce	7 ________der
2 ________cide	5 ________cuss	8 ________pend
3 ________sent	6 ________plain	9 ________vide

B **What are these people? Fill in the words (adjectives).**
Was sind diese Menschen? Tragen Sie die Eigenschaftswörter ein.

1 ___ ___ t ___ ___ ___ ___

2 ___ ___ ___ ___ r ___ ___ ___ ___

3 ___ ___ ___ ___

4 ___ ___ ___ ___ s ___ ___

5 ___ ___ r ___ ___ ___ ___

C **Conversations. Match the two parts of the conversations (1 – 6 and A – F).**
Gespräche. Ordnen Sie die zwei Teile (1 – 6 und A – F) der Gespräche einander zu.

1 "I think the firm is getting too big."
2 "My colleagues let me do all the work!"
3 "Can't we work more on Mondays and less on Fridays?"
4 "If you're late again tomorrow, you will have to go!"
5 "The boss wants to talk to us later. I think he's quite nervous."
6 "Are you going to come with us to the pub later or not?"

A "Why don't you complain to the boss?"
B "Good idea. Let's discuss it with the others."
C "I wonder what the problem is."
D "Yes, I agree."
E "Sorry, I haven't decided yet."
F "It won't happen again. I promise."

Going abroad

abroad	im/ins Ausland	to go abroad *(ins Ausland gehen)*
guest	Gast	
immigrant	Immigrant/in, Einwanderer/in	→ to immigrate *(einwandern)*
custom	Sitte, Brauch, Gewohnheit	
different	anders; andere/r/s	↔ same
another	ein/e andere/r/s	
to **adjust**	(sich) anpassen	
to **become**	werden	
to **miss**	vermissen	→ missing *(fehlend)*
to **join**	(sich) anschließen	
to **marry**	heiraten	
to **keep in touch**	in Kontakt bleiben	
to **give somebody a call**	jemanden anrufen	= to phone/ring/call somebody
Europe	Europa	→ European *(europäisch)*
Sweden	Schweden	→ Swedish
Swedish	Schwedisch	→ Sweden
Italy	Italien	→ Italian *(Italienisch)*
Spain	Spanien	→ Spanish *(Spanisch)*
Poland	Polen	→ Polish *(Polnisch)*
Indian	indisch	→ India *(Indien)*
travel agency	Reisebüro	→ to travel *(reisen)*
booking	Buchung	→ to book *(buchen)*

Customs

queuing; queue	Schlange stehen; (Warte-)Schlange	
to **form**	bilden	
small talk	Geplauder	= conversation
first name	Vorname	↔ last name *(Nachname)*
to **buy a round**	eine Runde ausgeben	
to **shake hands**	Hände schütteln, sich die Hand geben	
to **bow**	sich verbeugen	
to **take off**	ausziehen	↔ to put on
to **notice**	bemerken	

Jobs

builder	Bauarbeiter/in	→ to build *(bauen)*
baker	Bäcker/in	→ to bake *(backen)*
plumber	Installateur/in, Anlagenmechaniker/in für Sanitär-, Heizungs- und Klimatechnik	
electrician	Elektriker/in	→ electric *(elektrisch)*

Somebody or something is …

excited	aufgeregt	→ exciting *(aufregend)*
hard	hart	↔ soft *(weich)*
possible	möglich	↔ impossible *(unmöglich)*
necessary	nötig	
enough	genug	
special	besondere/r/s	

Food and drink

chips	Pommes frites	Chips are made out of potatoes.
marmalade	Marmelade aus Zitrusfrüchten	! jam *(Marmelade)*
canned soup	Suppe aus der Dose	
alcohol	Alkohol	
smell	Geruch	→ to smell *(riechen)*

Phrases

Say hi to … from me.	Grüße … von mir.

Symbole: = Synonym; ↔ Gegensatz; → Wortfamilie; ! Achtung

A **Take one piece out of each box of letters and put eight words together.**
Nehmen Sie ein Teil aus jedem Buchstabenkasten und fügen Sie acht Wörter zusammen.

~~mar~~	al	nec	po	ex	elec	ag	an

ssi	ci	~~ma~~	en	co	tric	oth	ess

ted	ble	~~lade~~	cy	ary	er	ian	hol

1 marmalade ______________________
2 ______________________
3 ______________________
4 ______________________
5 ______________________
6 ______________________
7 ______________________
8 ______________________

B **What are these flags? Read sentences 1–8 carefully and finish them.**
Was sind dies für Flaggen? Lesen Sie die Sätze 1–8 genau und vervollständigen Sie die Sätze.

1 
2 
3 
4 
5 
6 
7 
8 

1 This is the ______________________ flag.
2 This is the flag of ______________________.
3 This is the flag of ______________________.
4 It's the ______________________ flag.
5 This is the flag of ______________________.
6 This is the flag of ______________________.
7 This is the ______________________ flag.
8 This is the flag of ______________________.

C **Complete the sentences with the right word.**
Vervollständigen Sie die Sätze mit dem richtigen Wort.

1 When a person comes into a country and wants to stay there, he or she often is an ______________________.
2 When something is not like other things, you call it ______________________.
3 A lot of people ______________________ when they know that they want to be together for a very long time.
4 In Britain you join a ______________________ when you have to wait together with other people.
5 When people just talk about the weather or sports, you call the conversation "______________________".
6 A ______________________ is a person who repairs showers, for example.

So geht's …
10 Tipps zum Englischlernen

TIPP 1

Grammatik

Kaum jemand paukt gerne Grammatik, doch führt kein Weg daran vorbei. Die unregelmäßigen Verben sind dabei die halbe Miete. Wenn Sie die „draufhaben", fallen Ihnen die Zeiten sowie indirekte Rede, Aktiv / Passiv und *if*-Sätze viel leichter. Nehmen Sie sich jeden Tag ein Verb vor. Überlegen Sie auch, wie sich Verben in Gruppen zusammenfassen lassen (zum Beispiel *dr***i***nk-dr***a***nk-dr***u***nk* und *s***i***ng-s***a***ng-s***u***ng*).

Und wie wäre es, wenn Sie sich einmal die Woche hinsetzen und vier (beliebige) Sätze aus der aktuellen **Unit** abschreiben? Auch so prägt sich Grammatik ein!

TIPP 2

Projektarbeit/Gruppenarbeit:

Erfolgreiche Projekt- und Gruppenarbeit braucht Regeln:

- Legen Sie exakt fest, was Sie erarbeiten möchten. Fassen Sie das Thema nicht zu weit, sonst verlieren Sie leicht den Überblick.
- Als Nächstes: Planen Sie die einzelnen Arbeitsschritte. Das ist besonders wichtig, wenn Sie in einer Gruppe arbeiten. Wo finden Sie die notwendigen Informationen? Wer macht was bis wann?
- In welcher Form präsentieren Sie Ihre Ergebnisse? Referat? Plakat? Website? Klären Sie solche Fragen frühzeitig, um dann gezielt und effektiv arbeiten zu können.

TIPP 3

Umgang mit Lese- und Hörtexten

Lassen Sie sich von längeren Lese- und Hörtexten nicht verrückt machen. Und greifen Sie nicht gleich zum Wörterbuch. Beachten Sie stattdessen folgende Tipps:

- Vor dem ersten Lesen / Hören: Was verraten Überschriften und Bilder über den Inhalt des Textes? Mutmaßen Sie, worum es geht, das hilft beim anschließenden Verstehen.
- Lesen oder hören Sie den Text als Nächstes ein- oder zweimal, ohne an einzelnen Wörtern hängen zu bleiben. Völlig normal, wenn Sie nicht gleich alles verstehen.
- Danach erst ist Detailverständnis gefragt. Bevor Sie das Wörterbuch zücken, überlegen Sie, ob Sie einzelne Wörter, Ausdrücke, ganze Sätze, nicht doch aus dem Zusammenhang verstehen können. Dies ist eine ganz eigene Fähigkeit, aber wie alle anderen auch kann sie trainiert werden!

TIPP 4

Vokabellernen

Lernen Sie regelmäßig Vokabeln, nicht erst am Ende der *Unit* oder kurz vor der Arbeit. Fünf Vokabeln jeden Tag bringen mehr als eine lange Liste auf einmal.

Und noch etwas: Stellen Sie Wörter zu Wortfeldern zusammen, z. B. alle Wörter zum Thema **job** oder alle zum Wortfeld **internet**. Unser Gehirn lernt und erinnert sich leichter, wenn das Gelernte in Gruppen abgespeichert wird.

Lernen Sie Vokabeln im Zusammenhang, d.h. in einem kurzen Satz oder einer Wendung. Dann müssen Sie später nicht erst überlegen, wie es verwendet wird.
Beispiel: **home – at home – to go home**.

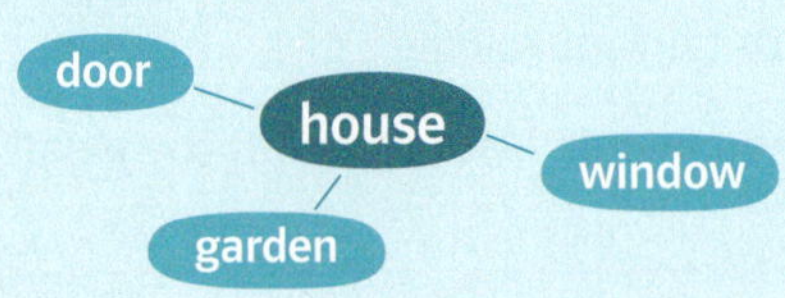

TIPP 5

Sprechen und Schreiben

Wetten, Sie finden Lesen und Hören auf Englisch einfacher als Sprechen und Schreiben? Das geht den meisten Leuten so. Der Schlüssel zum Erfolg: **KISS** = **K**eep **I**t **S**hort and **S**imple.
Vermeiden Sie lange und komplizierte Sätze, die Sie Wort für Wort ins Englische übersetzen. Konzentrieren Sie sich stattdessen auf einfache, knappe Sätze, bei denen Sie sich sicher fühlen. Lieber einfach und richtig als kompliziert und falsch.

K I S S

TIPP 6

Wörterbucharbeit

Ein zweisprachiges Wörterbuch ist wichtig, hat aber seine Tücken! Denn meistens bietet es mehrere Übersetzungen, und woran erkennt man die richtige? Am besten: Schlagen Sie die Übersetzung, für die Sie sich entschieden haben, als Gegenbeweis in der anderen Hälfte des Wörterbuchs nach.

TIPP 7

Klassenarbeiten und Prüfungen

- Fangen Sie rechtzeitig mit dem Lernen an, aber hören Sie auch rechtzeitig wieder auf. Nicht bis unmittelbar vor der Arbeit lernen!
- Während der Arbeit: Lesen Sie die Aufgabenstellung genau durch. Sie verschenken unnötig Punkte, wenn Sie nicht auf das antworten, was gefragt ist.
- Auch wenn's nervt: Lesen Sie die Arbeit mindestens einmal durch, bevor Sie sie abgeben. Irgendwas findet man immer!

TIPP 8

Wie hält man ein Referat?

Das A und O eines guten Referats: Sagen Sie Ihrem Publikum, worüber Sie sprechen werden (**Today I'd like to talk about ...**), sprechen Sie dann darüber und fassen Sie anschließend zusammen, was Sie gerade gesagt haben!

Setzen Sie visuelle Hilfen ein. Denn:
Wir lernen zu 80 % über das Sehen, nur zu 20 % über das Hören. Schreiben Sie Stichwörter an die Tafel, bereiten Sie eine Folie mit Bildern / Grafiken vor. Davon profitieren nicht nur Ihre Zuhörer, sondern auch Sie – denn so prägt sich der Ablauf Ihres Referats besser bei Ihnen ein.

TIPP 9

Mein Hobby? Englisch.

Englisch begegnet man heute überall – auf Kinoplakaten, in Zeitschriften, im Internet, in der Werbung, im Fernsehen, in Popsongs. Sperren Sie Augen und Ohren auf. Versuchen Sie z.B. Ihr aktuelles Lieblingslied zu verstehen oder schalten Sie, wenn Sie einen Film auf DVD schauen, auf die englische Spur um.

chips **pop song** **hamburger** **computer** **jeans**

TIPP 10

Und zum Schluss ...

Ein kluger Kopf hat einmal gesagt, mit dem Sprachenlernen sei es wie mit dem Autofahren: Übung macht den Meister! Wir können die Theorie noch so gut beherrschen, es ist erst die Praxis, die uns zu guten Autofahrern macht. Auch eine Sprache müssen Sie üben und üben, bis es irgendwann wie von selbst geht und Sie kaum noch Fehler machen. Und denken Sie daran: So schwer ist das alles nicht, das haben schon andere vor Ihnen geschafft!

A1.1 Unit 1 A bad day for BigDadDave

Here's a busy office. Lots of people work here. They answer the phone, they write to customers or they fill out forms.
And here's Dave. He's 21. He likes music. He's a rapper in his free time. He always has his MP3 player with him. He listens to it on his way to the office every morning. When he arrives at his desk, he takes his MP3 player off and puts it away.
At work, he phones customers every day. He's usually very good at his job. Mr Taylor, the boss, is pleased with him. His colleagues like him too. They know he raps and they know his rapper name, BigDadDave. Everybody calls him BigDad. But today something terrible happens. Listen.

Dave	… know him maybe, but you no good to show me baby …
Mary	Hi, BigDad. You're late today. You must phone Ms Francis at the Tradex company right away.
Dave	Hi, Mary. Just let me listen to this song. Tradex can wait.
Mary	No, they can't. Phone them now, please. Mr Taylor is angry already.
Dave	OK, OK. … now you step back …
Reception	Good morning. Tradex. How can I help you?
Dave	Er, I'd like to speak to Ms Francis, please.
Reception	OK. Please hold the line. I'll put you through.
Dave	… now listen to me: Yo, man!
Ms Francis	Who is this? Tell me who you are!
Dave	Sorry, Ms Francis. This is Dave McCoy from Grantly and Company. I want to …
Ms Francis	Be quiet. Who do you think you are? I'm phoning your boss – now.
Dave	Oh no!
Mary	What's the problem, BigDad?
Dave	Don't ask. I think I've got a new name.
Mary	A new name?
Dave	Yes. From now on you can call me BigBadDave.

A1.3 Unit 2 Terrible Tom

The people who work at Barker's Garage are good colleagues. They often go out together after work.
And they all get together when it's somebody's birthday – normally. Listen.

Tom	Sales department, Tom speaking. Hello.
Patty	Hello, Tom. It's Patty, your favourite colleague.
Tom	Oh, hello, Patty.
Patty	How are things? Do all your customers want to buy the new Invista?
Tom	Yes, they do. It's the best car in the world. And I'm the best salesman, of course. Do you want a test drive with me?
Patty	Ha, ha! You're terrible, Tom. Listen. It's Melinda's birthday today and …
Tom	Melinda? Do I know her?
Patty	Yes, you do! Long, blonde hair – my friend Melinda.
Tom	Ah, THAT Melinda! Does she need a new car?
Patty	Tom, stop it!
Tom	Sorry, Patty. So, what about Melinda?
Patty	It's her birthday today, so there's a meeting in the canteen at 1 o'clock to give Melinda her birthday present and have lunch together. And tonight it's drinks in the pub.
Tom	OK, what do you want me to do?
Patty	Just come to the canteen, be nice to Melinda – and give me two pounds for her present.
Tom	OK, thanks, Patty. See you later.

Two o'clock in the canteen …

Colleague	Time to get back to work. See you this evening, Melinda.
Melinda	Yes, great. And thank you all for the wonderful present.
Tom	Oh there you all are! Er, happy birthday, er, …
Patty	Melinda.
Tom	… Melinda. Sorry I'm late. Didn't you say 'a meeting in the pub', Patty?
Patty	No, Tom. We're in the pub this evening. But why didn't you come here earlier?
Tom	Well, what does a car salesman do? He sells cars! I've just sold another Invista – in the pub!

Patty That's great, Tom. Listen, everybody. Tom wants to celebrate the sale of another car and say sorry to Melinda for missing her birthday lunch. See you all for drinks at the pub at seven o'clock. And do you know who's paying, Tom?
Tom Melinda?
Patty No. You!

A1.6 Unit 3 The pizza problem

Paul and Tina are colleagues in a big shop. It's Friday evening and they're cooking at Tina's place. Paul has brought two pizzas. Listen.

Tina I'm making us a nice salad. Can you do the pizzas, please, Paul? The oven is on already.
Paul Of course. I'm quite a good cook, you know.
Tina OK, OK. Just hurry up, Paul. I'm very hungry. The salad won't be enough.
Paul I'm reading what it says on the packet. OK. 200 degrees, 11 minutes. … In you go, pizzas.
Tina Let's have a drink in the living room while we're waiting. Oh, and we have to talk about a birthday present for Harry. He'll be 21 next week.
Paul 21! You know, I've known him since he was 11. And now he's 21 …

…

Paul Thanks, Tina. That's a very nice drink. Where are you working this month?
Tina I'm helping out in the sports department. And you?
Paul I'm working in the TV department. It's boring. But next month it's the music department for me. That's much more interesting.
Tina Right. And I'm hoping I can stay in the sports department. It's …

…

Paul … in the mornings. Hey. Twenty minutes. Our pizzas are almost ready.
Tina Twenty minutes?! Are you sure?
Paul Well, it says twenty-one minutes on the packet actually.
Tina Let me check the packet. – I knew it! It isn't 21, it's 11 minutes!
Paul Oh no! Quick!
Tina Too late. I'm opening all the windows. What a smell!
Paul And I'll throw these black pizzas away. I'm so sorry. What was I thinking?
Tina You were thinking about Harry's birthday – remember? I told you he's 21 on Saturday. I think it's time to make a phone call.
Paul A phone call?
Tina Yes, to the pizza service.

A1.10 Unit 4 Rent-a-Wreck

Mila Hi, Sue! Are you back from your holiday already?
Sue Hello, Mila. Yes, it went much too quickly.
Mila How was it?
Sue Have you got some time? Let's go into this café and I can tell you. It was quite exciting actually.
Mila OK.

…

Sue … and poor Tim was in hospital. He couldn't pick me up, and he couldn't show me Colorado in his car. So there I was, all alone at Denver Airport. I didn't want to fly back to England. But I didn't have a car. And I didn't have much money.
So first of all I went to the car rental desk and asked for their smallest camper van. The price was terrible! OK, I thought, I can sleep in a normal car, if it's big enough. That was the next shock. Big cars cost big money in the USA! So then I asked about a small car – and do you know what? They didn't have one! "We don't drive small cars out here," the man at the desk said. "What about a motorbike?" I asked angrily. "No problem," he said. "Could I just see your driving licence, please?"
I gave him my licence and he said "Sorry. Your driving licence doesn't cover you for the bikes we have – they're big bikes, of course." "Yes," I said. "Of course!"
Mila Poor you.
Sue Well, what could I do? I took a bus into downtown Denver and walked around. In a shabby little street I saw a garage. There was a sign outside that said "Don't pay full prices for a big, new rental car. Rent a Wreck!" – And that's what I did! I paid for two weeks' rental of a "wreck", a little car that looked really old and dirty.
Mila And did you like the car?
Sue Yes, I did. I got in and started driving. I felt really happy. The engine was noisy and the car wasn't very fast, but the brakes worked well, so it was OK for me. First of all I went to Boulder to visit my

brother Tim in hospital. He looked terrible. Both his legs were broken! "That must have been a bad accident. Were you driving your own car?" I asked him. And he said, "Yes, my brakes suddenly didn't work. That's the problem with modern cars and their electronic systems." "That's terrible," I said. "I'm so glad that this can't happen to me – my rental car is from Rent-a-Wreck in Denver …"

A1.14 Unit 5 Forget the interview

Jenny Williams Good morning. Metronorma, Human Resources Department.
Peter Townsend Hi. It's about my interview.
Jenny Williams And your name is …?
Peter Townsend Pete, er, Peter, Peter Townsend.
Jenny Williams And how can I help you, Mr Townsend.
Peter Townsend Well, as I said, it's about my interview. It's on Friday.
Jenny Williams Yes. I can see it on my computer screen. Friday, 9 a.m.
Peter Townsend Well, that's the problem, you see. I don't know about your boss, Mr … eh … Williams, but I really wouldn't like an interview at 9 a.m. I'm usually still in bed then.
Jenny Williams So you aren't good at working hard in the morning?
Peter Townsend In the morning? Heavens no! I usually only get back from the pub at around midnight. And then I'm tired all day. I don't really wake up till the evening – you know, in my free time. But don't tell your boss that.
Jenny Williams Don't tell my boss. I see.
Peter Townsend So could you ask your boss if I could have the interview after 3 p.m.? That would be great. And what do you think I should wear? You're his assistant and you're probably wearing a suit, but I don't have to dress well, do I? I was thinking of coming in jeans and a T-shirt – a clean one, of course. That will be OK, won't it? I just haven't got time to go out and buy a jacket and trousers.
Jenny Williams Or even a suit?
Peter Townsend A suit! Me in a suit? Never!
Jenny Williams Well, I've got some news for you, Mr Townsend. You won't need a suit, you won't even need a clean T-shirt, because you won't have an interview on Friday.
Peter Townsend What?! But your boss, Mr J. Williams, invited me to an interview!
Jenny Williams Forget the interview. J. Williams – that's me, Jenny Williams. The boss. Well, you can go back to bed now. It's only 11 o'clock in the morning. Too early for you. Goodbye. Or perhaps I should say "Good night"!

A1.16 Unit 6 Ask Aysha

Aysha Hi again. This is Aysha Patel. You're listening to KFM's express phone-in show, *Ask Aysha*. Our topic tonight is *What job should I do?* And here's our next caller, Sally from Rochdale. Hi, Sally. How can I help you?
Sally Well, I've just come back from the Formula One race at the Nürburgring in Germany. So, er, I'm really interested in cars. I'm still at college but I'm looking for a job. My parents say I should look for office work. I've worked in an office before, in the school holidays. But I really want to be a car mechanic. I've just repaired my brother's motorbike for him and I loved it. My brother was pleased too! But everybody says only boys can be car mechanics. What should I do?
Aysha Don't listen to them, Sally. Boys and girls can do the same jobs. You are you. Do what you're good at. Look for a job at a local garage – and I don't mean in the office there!
Sally OK. Thanks, Aysha.
Aysha And our next caller, please. It's Greg, isn't it?
Greg That's right. Hi, Aysha. I left school last summer and, er, I haven't found a job yet.
Aysha What kind of job are you looking for, Greg?
Greg That's the problem. I don't know. I'm not really interested in anything – except watching TV. Seriously, I love watching shows about real people. You should see some of the clothes that people wear! Did you see "The Lunch Show" yesterday? That man in the green shirt and orange trousers? I mean you really shouldn't wear …

Aysha Stop! Stop! Listen to yourself. You ARE interested in something – clothes! Look for a job at a fashion shop or department store or …

Greg I've never thought about that before. You're right! Thanks, Aysha.

Aysha And our next caller is Paula. She wants to be a chef. Right, Paula?

Paula Hi, Aysha. That's right. But there's a problem. I can't cook and …

Aysha Sorry, you want to be a chef, but you can't cook? That IS a problem.

Paula No, well, what I mean is, I can't cook AND talk at the same time. I can only cook. People love my meals. I just can't explain things like the famous TV chefs.

Aysha But that's fine, Paula. You've just said what's most important: People love your cooking. Forget the talking – just do the cooking. Let's take another music break …

A1.18

Unit 7 Going abroad for work

Nils Hi. This is Nils Weber. Who's speaking, please?

Sandra Hi, Nils. This is Sandra, Sandra Jones from Ferguson's Hotel and Restaurant. I just wanted to find out if our new chef has arrived safely in England.

Nils Good morning, Sandra. That's nice of you to phone. Everything is fine, thanks. I've just arrived in Dover. I'm still on the ship at the moment. I think I'm going to have breakfast somewhere before I start the long drive up to Manchester.

Sandra I see. Great! Take your time. Driving too fast can get very expensive here. It's not like on one of your German autobahns!

Nils Don't worry, Sandra. I'm going to drive nice and slowly. And I'm going to stop a few times on the way up to you. My Navi … er … my satnav says it's going to take five hours to drive from Dover to Manchester.

Sandra If you're lucky! The traffic reports are very bad. It's going to take you longer than five hours today, I'm afraid. But you have a free day tomorrow and you aren't going to start work here till Monday, so it doesn't really matter.

Nils Really? I'm glad to hear that. I'm going to listen to English radio and enjoy the drive. And I'm going to think about what I'm going to cook on my first day. What about sauerkraut, bratwurst and fried potatoes as a lunch special? Perhaps you could even find some German beer to go with it.

Sandra Yeah, well … Listen, I'm not sure if that's a good idea. Perhaps you could try …

Nils I was only joking! I know that people are going to want something nice and light at lunchtime. I think I'm going to cook something Italian.

Sandra That sounds good. Our new German chef is going to cook something Italian! Why not? So you're going to arrive some time this evening. If it's past six o'clock, you'll find us in the restaurant. Just come there for the key to your flat – and for a meal, of course.

Nils OK. I'm going to go down to the car deck now.

Sandra Sure. One more thing, Nils. When you leave the port of Dover there's a big sign. Please read it carefully.

Nils A big sign? What does it say?

Sandra Links fahren.

Nils Don't worry, Sandra! Natürlich werde ich links fahren! Of course I'm going to drive on the left! See you tonight then.

Sandra Good luck. Bye.

1 Das *simple present*

A Allgemein

Das *simple present* verwende ich:

- um zu sagen, was ich regelmäßig mache.
- um zu sagen, was gewöhnlich der Fall ist.

B Mit *sometimes, often,* usw.

Das *simple present* wird oft mit Wörtern wie *usually, normally, sometimes, often, always, never* verwendet. Diese Wörter (Adverbien) stehen immer:

- **vor** einem Vollverb.
- **nach** einer Form von *to be*.

*I **usually** get up at 7 a.m.*

*I **often** watch TV in the evenings.*

*I'm **always** happy on Fridays.*

C Bildung: Aussagen

Das *simple present* wird aus der Grundform des Verbs (Infinitiv ohne *to*) gebildet. Nach *he/she/it* endet das Verb immer auf -*s* oder -*es*!

1. An die meisten Verben wird einfach -*s* angehängt.
2. Die Endung -*es* wird bei Verben benutzt, die auf *s, ss, x, ch* oder *sh* enden (z. B. *to finish*), da es schwer wäre, nur ein -*s* auszusprechen.
3. Auch die Verben *go* und *do* enden mit -*es*.
4. Ein Sonderfall sind Verben, die auf -*y* enden: *to tidy* → *he tid**ies***.

1. to work	2. to finish
I work you work he/she/it work**s** we work you work they work	I finish you finish he/she/it finish**es** we finish you finish they finish

3. to go	4. to tidy
I go you go he/she/it go**es** we go you go they go	I tidy you tidy he/she/it tid**ies** we tidy you tidy they tidy

D Bildung: Fragen und Verneinungen

- Fragen im *simple present* werden mit *do* (bei *he/she/it*: *does*) gebildet.
- Verneinungen bildet man mit *don't* (nach *he/she/it*: *doesn't*).

Vorsicht!

Nach *does/doesn't* kommt immer die Grundform des Verbs:

Does he work? (! Does he ~~works~~?)

She doesn't work. (! She doesn't ~~works~~.)

Fragen	Verneinungen
Do I work? Do you work? Does he/she/it work? Do we work? Do you work? Do they work?	I don't work you don't work he/she/it doesn't wor**k** we don't work you don't work they don't work

2 Das *present progressive*

A Allgemein
Das *present progressive* verwende ich, um zu sagen, was ich gerade mache. Ich benutze es auch, um ein Bild zu beschreiben. Es wird häufig mit Zeitangaben wie *at the moment* und *right now* verwendet.

*I'm **reading** this text at the moment.*

What can you see in this photo?
*– A hairdresser. Right now, she**'s cutting** a customer's hair.*

B Bildung: Aussagen
Das *present progressive* wird mit einer Form von *to be* und dem Verb + *-ing* gebildet.

C Bildung: Fragen und Verneinungen
Fragen und Verneinungen werden mit den Frage- und Verneinungsformen von *to be* gebildet.

I'm you're he's/she's/it's we're you're they're	working	I'm not working she isn't working Am I working? Are you working? Are they working?

Verb + *-ing*: Schreibregeln
- An die meisten Verben wird einfach *-ing* angehängt: *work – work**ing**, do – do**ing***.
- Verben, die auf *-e* enden, verlieren das *-e*: *us**e** – us**ing**, danc**e** – danc**ing***.
- Kurze Verben, die auf einen Vokal und einen Konsonanten (außer *-y*, *-w* und *-x*) enden, verdoppeln den Konsonanten: *cu**t** – cu**tting*** (ABER: *pla**y** – pla**ying***).
- Längere Verben, die auf einen Vokal und einen Konsonanten enden, verdoppeln den Konsonanten nicht: *visi**t** – visi**ting**, delive**r** – delive**ring***. (Ausnahmen: *trave**ll**ing, begi**nn**ing*)
- Bei Verben, die auf *-ie* enden, wird *-ie* zu *-y*: ***die** – **dying***

***Simple present* oder *present progressive*?**

This is Patrick. He lives in England. He works in a supermarket five days a week.

It's 8.30 in the morning. Patrick is going to the supermarket by bus.

3 Das *simple past*

A Allgemein

Ich verwende das *simple past*, um zu sagen, was in der Vergangenheit geschah.
Es wird häufig mit Zeitangaben wie *yesterday, in 1990, last week* und *3 years ago* benutzt.

B Bildung: Aussagen

- Regelmäßige Verben bilden das *simple past* mit *-ed*. Diese Form bleibt in allen Personen gleich.
- Unregelmäßige Verben haben Sonderformen im *simple past* (eine Liste finden Sie auf der vorderen Umschlagseite, innen). Diese Formen (außer bei *to be*) bleiben ebenfalls in allen Personen gleich.

regelmäßig	unregelmäßig	
to work	**to go**	**to be**
I worked	I went	I **was**
you worked	you went	you **were**
he worked	he went	he was
she worked	she went	she was
it worked	it went	it was
we worked	we went	we were
you worked	you went	you were
they worked	they went	they were

C Bildung: Fragen und Verneinungen

- Fragen im ***simple past*** werden in allen Personen mit *did* gebildet.
- Verneinungen bildet man durchgehend mit *didn't.*
- *to be* bildet Fragen und Verneinungen im ***simple past*** mit eigenen Formen.

Vorsicht!
Nach *did/didn't* steht immer die Grundform des Verbs:
Did he work? (! Did he ~~worked~~?)
She didn't work. (! She didn't ~~worked~~.)

Fragen	Verneinungen
Did I work? Did you work? Did he/she/it work? Did we work? Did you work? Did they work?	I didn't work you didn't work he/she/it didn't work we didn't work you didn't work they didn't work
to be	
Was I? Were you? Was he/she/it? Were we/you/they?	I wasn't you weren't he/she/it wasn't we/you/they/weren't

Verb + *-ed*: Schreibregeln

- An die meisten Verben wird einfach *-ed* angehängt: *work – work**ed**.*
- An Verben, die auf *-e* enden, hängt man nur *-d* an: *use – use**d**, dance – dance**d**.*
- Kurze Verben, die auf einen Vokal *(a, e, i o, u)* und einen Konsonanten (außer *-y, -w* und *-x*) enden, verdoppeln den Konsonanten: *shop – shop**ped**, jog – jog**ged**.*
- Längere Verben, die auf einen Vokal und einen Konsonanten enden, verdoppeln den Konsonanten nicht: *visit – visit**ed**, deliver – deliver**ed**.* (Ausnahme: *travel**led***)
- Bei Verben, die auf *-y* enden, wird *-y* zu *-i*: *stud**y** – stud**ied**.*

4 Das *present perfect*

A Allgemein

Ich verwende das *present perfect*, um zu sagen, was gerade eben (oder noch nicht) geschehen ist. Ich sage damit auch, was schon einmal (oder noch nie) gemacht wurde.

B Bildung: Aussagen

Das *present perfect* wird mit einer Form von *to have* und der 3. Form des Verbs (Partizip Perfekt) gebildet.

- Regelmäßige Verben (z. B. *to work*) bilden ihre 3. Form mit *-ed*.
- Unregelmäßige Verben (z. B. *to go*) haben Sonderformen, die in der Liste auf der vorderen Umschlagseite (innen) zu finden sind.

I have (I've) you have (you've) he has (he's) she has (she's) it has (it's) we have (we've) you have (you've) they have (they've)	worked gone

C Bildung: Fragen und Verneinungen

Fragen und Verneinungen werden mit Frage- und Verneinungsformen von *to have* + 3. Form des Verbs gebildet.

Have you worked? Has he worked?
I haven't worked you haven't worked he/she/it hasn't worked we/you/they haven't worked

5 Das Futur: *will*

A Allgemein

Ich verwende *will*, um zu sagen, was ich in der Zukunft tun werde.

*I'**ll have** a family in 10 years.*
*She **won't leave** her job when she has a family.*

B Bildung

- **Aussagen** werden mit *will* + Grundform des Verbs gebildet. Die Kurzform (*'ll*) wird fast immer beim Sprechen und häufig auch beim Schreiben verwendet.
- **Fragen** bildet man, indem man *will* und das Subjekt umstellt. Hier sind die Kurzformen nicht möglich.
- **Verneinungen** werden mit *won't* + Grundform des Verbs gebildet.

I will (I'll) come you will (you'll) come he will (he'll) come she will (she'll) come it will (it'll) come we will (we'll) come you will (you'll) come they will (they'll) come	Will I come? Will you come? Will he come? Will she come? Will it come? Will we come? Will you come? Will they come?
I/you won't come he/she/it won't come we/you/they won't come	

6 Das Futur: *going to*

A Allgemein

Ich verwende *going to*, um über Pläne und Absichten zu sprechen: *I'm going to buy a new jacket* entspricht etwa auf Deutsch: „Ich habe vor, eine neue Jacke zu kaufen."

***I'm going to** look for a new job next month.*
***Are** you **going to** leave home?*

B Bildung

- **Aussagen** bildet man mit *to be* + *going to* + Hauptverb.
- **Fragen** bildet man mit den Frageformen von *to be* + *going to* + Hauptverb.
- Für **Verneinungen** benutzt man die Verneinung von *to be* + *going to* + Hauptverb.

I'm you're he's/she's/it's we're/you're/they're	going to	work
Am I Are you Is he/she/it Are we/you/they	going to	work?
I'm not you aren't he/she/it isn't we/you/they aren't	going to	work

7 Die Verben *to be* und *to have*

A Allgemein

To be und *to have* kommen sehr häufig vor. Man braucht diese Verben auch zur Bildung einiger Zeitformen, deshalb sind sie besonders wichtig. Bei *to be* und *to have* gibt es einige Unregelmäßigkeiten, die man kennen sollte.

***Are** you English? – Yes, I **am**.*
*Peter **has got** a sister.*

B Bildung

***to be*:**

- Das Verb *to be* hat die Formen *am*, *is* und *are* im *simple present* und *was* und *were* im *simple past*.
- Die Verneinung bildet man mit *not*.
- Die Formen von *to be* werden oft als Kurzformen verwendet.
  Vorsicht! Apostroph nicht vergessen!

simple present	Kurzformen	Verneinung	Kurzformen Verneinung
I am	I'm	I am not	I'm not
you are	you're	you are not	you're not **oder** you aren't
he/she/it is	he's/she's/it's	he/she/it is not	he's/she's/it's not **oder** he/she/it isn't
we are	we're	we are not	we're not **oder** we aren't
you are	you're	you are not	you're not **oder** you aren't
they are	they're	they are not	they're not **oder** they aren't

simple past	**Verneinung (Kurzform)**
I was	I wasn't
you were	you weren't
he/she/it was	he/she/it wasn't
we were	we weren't
you were	you weren't
they were	they weren't

***to have*:**
- Das Verb *to have* hat nur die Ausnahmeform *has* (in der dritten Person im *simple present*).
- Auch die Formen von *to have* werden oft als Kurzformen verwendet.

Vorsicht!
Die Form *have got* wird nur im *simple present* benutzt.
Die Verneinung bildet man mit *not*.
Das *simple past* von *have got* ist *had* (ohne *got*).
Die Verneinung ist *didn't have*.

simple present	**Kurzformen**	**Verneinung *have got***
I have (got)	I've (got)	I haven't got
you have (got)	you've (got)	you haven't got
he/she/it has (got)	he's/she's/it's (got)	he/she/it hasn't got
we have (got)	we've (got)	we haven't got
you have (got)	you've (got)	you haven't got
they have (got)	they've (got)	they haven't got

simple past:
I/you/he/she/it/we/you/they **had**

Verneinung:
I/you/he/she/it/we/you/they **didn't have**

C Fragen

Anders als bei normalen Verben bildet man Fragen mit *to be* und *have got* durch Satzumstellung.
Ausnahme: Wenn *to have* ohne *got* verwendet wird, wird es als normales Verb behandelt!

Lucia **is** nice. → **Is** Lucia nice?
Tom **has got** a new car. → **Has** Tom **got** a new car?
We **had** an accident. → **Did** you **have** an accident?

D There is/are ...

Mit *there is (there's)* oder *there are (simple past: there was/were)* sage ich, dass es etwas gibt (gab).
Im Englischen braucht man diese Formulierung sehr oft.

There's a new club in town.
There were lots of people there last night.

8 Das Passiv

A Allgemein:
Passivsätze betonen, **was** getan wird (nicht **wer** etwas tut) – die Handlung steht im Vordergrund.

Meals **are cooked** in the canteen.

B Bildung
Das Passiv wird mit *to be* + 3. Form des Verbs (Partizip Perfekt) gebildet.

simple present		simple past	
I'm		I was	
you're		you were	
he's		he was	
she's		she was	
it's	**made**	it was	**made**
we're		we were	
you're		you were	
they're		they were	

They delivered oranges to the supermarket yesterday.

Too many oranges were delivered to the supermarket yesterday!

9 *If*-Sätze (Bedingungssätze)

A Allgemein
Ein Bedingungssatz besteht aus einem *if*-Teil und einem Hauptsatz. Der *if*-Teil beschreibt eine Bedingung. Der Hauptsatz drückt aus, was (nicht) passieren wird, wenn diese Bedingung erfüllt wird.

B Bildung
- Bedingungssätze können entweder mit dem *if*-Teil oder mit dem Hauptsatz beginnen.
- Beginnt ein Satz mit dem *if*-Teil, dann steht immer ein Komma vor dem Hauptsatz.

If + simple present	will (not) + verb
If you go to the party,	you'll see Mitch.

will (not) + verb	if + simple present
I won't leave Germany	if I find a good job here.

10 Relativsätze

A Allgemein
Wenn ich Sachen oder Personen näher beschreiben will, benutze ich Relativpronomen wie *who*, *which* oder *that*.

***The woman who** is helping him is Frau Bliscz.*
***The document that** she has in her hand is Herr Krueger's letter.*

B *who, which* oder *that*?
- *who* für Personen
- *which* für Sachen
- *that* für Personen oder Sachen

Vorsicht!
Anders als im Deutschen steht kein Komma vor *who, which* und *that*.

*A passenger is a person **who** travels by plane.*
*A plane is a machine **which** carries people.*
*Ms Brown is the passenger **that** needs special help.*

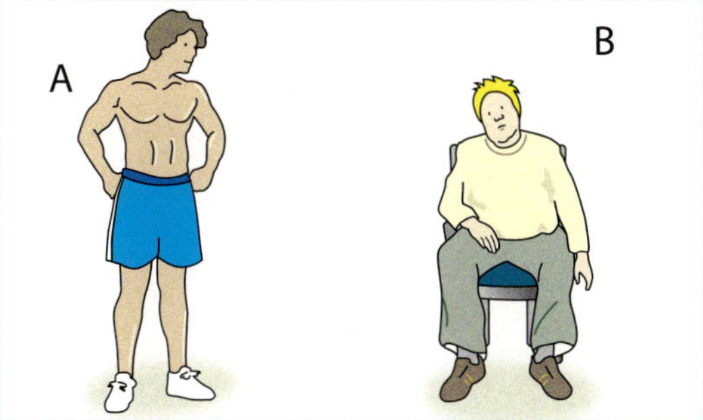

The guy who goes to a fitness club every day is A or B?

11 Adjektive

A Allgemein

Adjektive beschreiben Personen und Sachen. Sie stehen meist vor einem Substantiv oder nach *to be*.

*It is a **big** robot.*
*The robot is **big**.*

B Steigerung

- **Einsilbige Adjektive** werden mit *-er* und *-est* gesteigert.
- **Zweisilbige Adjektive**, die auf *-y* enden, werden mit *-ier* und *-iest* gesteigert.
- Bei **Vergleichen** benutzt man *than* (= als).

*Peter is **older** than Frank.*
*He is **the oldest**.*

*Susan is **prettier** than Tina.*
*Dana is **the prettiest**.*

- Die meisten anderen zweisilbigen Adjektive und alle **mehrsilbigen Adjektive** werden mit *more* und *most* gesteigert.

*John's house is **more modern** than Paul's.*
*Jackie's house is **the most modern** one in Brighton.*

*My car is **more expensive** than Melanie's.*
*Bob's car is **the most expensive**.*

- Bei **Vergleichen** von Personen und Sachen verwendet man *as … as* oder *not as … as*.

*Conny's trolley is **as big as** Frank's.*
*Sean's stereo is **not as good as** Naomi's.*

- Einige Adjektive haben **unregelmäßige Steigerungsformen**.

good	better	best
bad	worse	worst
much/many	more	most
little	less	least

*This jam is **the least expensive**.*

12 Adverbien

A Allgemein

Mit **Adverbien** sage ich, wie jemand etwas tut.

*The robot loads the lorries **quickly**.*

B Bildung

- Ein Adverb wird gebildet, indem *-ly* an das Adjektiv angehängt wird. →
- Bei Adjektiven mit der Endung *-y* wird das *-y* zu *-ily*. →
- Die Endung *-le* wird zu *-ly*. →
- *-ic* wird zu *-ically*. →
- Das Adverb von *good* ist *well*. →

Adjektiv	Adverb
quick	quick**ly**
easy	eas**ily**
simple	simp**ly**
automatic	automat**ically**
good	**well**

13 Überblick: Persönliche Fürwörter

Persönliche Fürwörter stehen für Dinge, Personen oder Tiere.
Sie ändern ihre Form, je nachdem, welche Funktion sie erfüllen.

Vorsicht!
Über einen Gegenstand spricht man nur mit *it* (nicht ~~*he/she*~~).

Wer?							
I	**you**	**he**	**she**	**it**	**we**	**you**	**they**
ich	du	er	sie	es	wir	ihr	sie
Wem? Wen?							
me	**you**	**him**	**her**	**it**	**us**	**you**	**them**
mir/mich	dir/dich	ihm/ihn	ihr/sie	ihm/es	uns	euch	ihnen/sie
Wessen?							
my	**your**	**his**	**her**	**its**	**our**	**your**	**their**
mein	dein	sein	ihr	sein	unser	euer	ihr

14 Überblick: Besitz angeben

Eine Person → Paul**'s** book
Mehrere Personen → the student**s'** books
Sachen → the colour **of** the book

15 Gerundien

A Allgemein
Mit Gerundien spricht man über Tätigkeiten.
Sie werden wie Nomen verwendet.

***Singing** is my hobby.*

B Bildung
Gerundien werden aus Verb + *-ing* gebildet
(vgl. *present progressive*).

***Running** is great to keep fit.*

Videotraining: Englische Aussprache

Perfekte englische Aussprache leicht gemacht: Mit dem Lernprogramm zur englischen Lautschrift können Sie alle Laute einüben. Wählen Sie einfach in der Navigation rechts den entsprechenden Reiter (*Vowels* oder *Consonants*) aus und klicken Sie dann auf das gewünschte phonetische Symbol. Sprechen Sie die Wörter laut nach.

n633sn

Unter www.klett.de geben Sie einfach den Cool!-Code ein. Von dort aus können Sie die Webanwendung online starten.

Cool! compact dictionary zum Download

em2p3f

Im Internet steht die komplette Wortliste Deutsch – Englisch für Sie zum Download bereit. Geben Sie einfach den nebenstehenden Cool!-Code unter www.klett.de ein.

Talking vocabulary

i5ju5w

Außerdem finden Sie im Internet die vertonten Vokabeln der Units sowie die unregelmäßigen Verben als MP3-Dateien zum Download. Geben Sie hierfür den Cool!-Code der jeweiligen Unit bzw. den nebenstehenden Cool!-Code (für die Verben) unter www.klett.de ein.

Vokabeltraining

Zum vertiefenden Vokabellernen stehen Ihnen die Vokabeltrainingseiten *Vocabulary* (S. 98 – 111) zur Verfügung. Hier können die Vokabeln der sieben Units sowie zusätzliche Vokabeln zum jeweiligen Thema mit abwechslungsreichen Übungen trainiert werden.

Cool!-Codes

Im Internet stehen folgende Materialien für Sie zum Download bereit.
Geben Sie einfach den entsprechenden Cool!-Code unter www.klett.de ein.

		Cool!-Code
Units 1 – 7 Zu jeder Unit finden Sie hier – das **Talking vocabulary** – die vertonten Vokabeln der Unit als MP3-Datei – **Üben interaktiv** – Multimediale und interaktive Online-Übungsaufgaben zu den Grammatikthemen der Unit	Unit 1	f6en95
	Unit 2	45j9ub
	Unit 3	3e84cu
	Unit 4	c6x6pv
	Unit 5	s6wi47
	Unit 6	uz76gm
	Unit 7	t96aj7
Unregelmäßige Verben – vertont, im MP3-Format. Abgedruckt finden Sie die unregelmäßigen Verben auf der vorderen inneren Umschlagseite.		i5ju5w
Cool! compact dictionary – die komplette Wortliste Deutsch – Englisch		em2p3f
Phonetic Alphabet – Videotraining zur englischen Aussprache		n633sn

A

a few months ago [ə ˌfju: 'mʌnθs‿əˌgəʊ]	vor ein paar Monaten	67
a year ago [ə 'jɪər‿əˌgəʊ]	vor einem Jahr	50
abroad [ə'brɔ:d]	im/ins Ausland	22, 78
accident ['æksɪdnt]	Unfall	43
accidentally [ˌaksɪ'dentlɪ]	versehentlich	87
ad [æd]	Anzeige	20
to **adjust** [ə'dʒʌst]	(sich) anpassen	82
advert ['ædvɜ:t]	Anzeige	32
advertised ['ædvətaɪzd]	ausgeschrieben	59
advertising ['ædvətaɪzɪŋ]	Werbung	10
advice [əd'vaɪs]	Ratschlag	46
after that [ˌɑ:ftə 'ðæt]	danach	44
to **agree** [ə'gri:]	zustimmen	21
to **agree** [ə'gri:]	sich einig sein	27
alcohol ['ælkəhɒl]	Alkohol	56
all over the world [ɔ:l ˌəʊvə ðə 'wɜ:ld]	überall auf der Welt	20
all the time [ˌɔ:lðə'taɪm]	die ganze Zeit	6
to **allow** [ə'laʊ]	erlauben	23
allowed [ə'laʊd]	erlaubt	8
almost ['ɔ:lməʊst]	beinahe, fast	8
along [ə'lɒŋ]	entlang	47
already [ɔ:l'redɪ]	schon, bereits	8
another [ə'nʌðə]	ein/e andere/r/s	80
to answer the phone [ˌɑ:nsə ðə 'fəʊn]	ans Telefon gehen	8
Anything else? [ˌenɪθɪŋ 'els]	Noch etwas?	34
anyway ['enɪweɪ]	überhaupt	70
application [ˌæplɪ'keɪʃn]	Bewerbung	56
to **apply (for)** [ə'plaɪ]	sich bewerben (um)	56
appointment [ə'pɔɪntmənt]	Termin, Verabredung	8
apprenticeship [ə'prentɪsʃɪp]	Lehre, Ausbildung	54
around [ə'raʊnd]	in der Nähe	8
as old as [əz 'əʊld‿əz]	so alt wie	32
to **ask somebody** [ɑ:sk]	jemanden bitten	10
attached [ə'tætʃt]	beigefügt, angehängt	59
to **avoid** [ə'vɔɪd]	vermeiden	10
awful ['ɔ:fəl]	furchtbar	32

B

baker ['beɪkə]	Bäcker/in	80
basic info [ˌbeɪsɪk 'ɪnfəʊ]	allgemeine Informationen	23
to **be a team player** [bi‿ə ˌti:m 'pleɪə]	teamfähig sein	59
to **be able** [bi‿'eɪbl]	in der Lage sein	59
to **be awake** [bi‿ə'weɪk]	wach sein	55
to **be lost** [bi 'lɒst]	sich verlaufen/ verirrt haben	47
to **become** [bɪ'kʌm]	werden	68
before [bɪ'fɔ:]	zuvor, schon einmal	66
to **believe** [bɪ'li:v]	glauben	51
to **bet** [bet]	wetten	32
between [bɪ'twi:n]	zwischen	27, 47
blouse [blaʊz]	Bluse	58
booking ['bʊkɪŋ]	Buchung	59
boot [bu:t]	Kofferraum	44
both [bəʊθ]	beide	6
to **bow** [baʊ]	sich verbeugen	83
boyfriend ['bɔɪfrend]	(fester) Freund	19
broadband ['brɔ:dbænd]	Breitband	32
builder ['bɪldə]	Bauarbeiter/in	78
building firm ['bɪldɪŋ ˌfɜ:m]	Baufirma	46
business card ['bɪznɪs ˌkɑ:d]	Visitenkarte	83
to buy a round [ˌbaɪ‿ə 'raʊnd]	eine Runde ausgeben	82
by the way [ˌbaɪ ðə 'weɪ]	übrigens	22

C

cable TV [ˌkeɪbl ˌti:'vi:]	Kabelfernsehen	32
call centre agent [ˌkɔ:lsentər‿'eɪdʒənt]	Callcenteragent/in	14
camper van ['kæmpə ˌvæn]	Wohnmobil	42
canned soup [ˌkænd 'su:p]	Suppe aus der Dose	56
canteen [kæn'ti:n]	Kantine	19
car mechanic ['kɑ: məˌkænɪk]	Automechaniker/in	54
car salesman ['kɑ: ˌseɪlzmn]	Autoverkäufer	68
career dream [kə'rɪə ˌdri:m]	Berufstraum	66
carrot ['kærət]	Möhre, Karotte	31
case [keɪs]	Behälter	44
cassette [kə'set]	Kassette	44
certainly ['sɜ:tnlɪ]	sicher, selbstverständlich	8
to change trains [tʃeɪndʒ 'treɪnz]	umsteigen	46
chauffeur ['ʃəʊfə]	Chauffeur/in, Fahrer/in	56
chef [ʃef]	Koch/Köchin	67
chips [tʃɪps]	Pommes frites	80
church [tʃɜ:tʃ]	Kirche	47
classmate ['klɑ:smeɪt]	Klassenkamerad/in	19
classy ['klɑ:sɪ]	edel, elegant	20
clear [klɪə]	klar, deutlich	10
clothes [kləʊðz]	Kleidung	11
coat [kəʊt]	Mantel, Jacke	8

colleague ['kɒli:g]	Kollege, Kollegin	19
collection [kə'lekʃn]	Sammlung	11
community [kə'mju:nətɪ]	Gemeinschaft	18
company ['kʌmpənɪ]	Firma	10
to **complain** [kəm'pleɪn]	sich beschweren	70
to **continue working** [kən,tɪnju:‿'wɜ:kɪŋ]	weiter arbeiten	70
conversation [,kɒnvə'seɪʃn]	Gespräch	68
to **count** [kaʊnt]	zählen	39
to **crash the car into something** ['kræʃ ,ɪntə]	mit dem Auto in etwas hineinkrachen	44
crazy ['kreɪzɪ]	verrückt	20
to **cross** [krɒs]	überqueren	47
cupboard ['kʌbəd]	Schrank	32
to **curl** [kɜ:l]	kräuseln, aufdrehen	8
current location [,kʌrənt ləʊ'keɪʃn]	derzeitiger Wohnort	23
custom ['kʌstəm]	Sitte, Brauch, Gewohnheit	82
customer ['kʌstəmə]	Kunde/Kundin	8
CV [,si:'vi:]	Lebenslauf	59
to **cycle** ['saɪkl]	Rad fahren	42

D

to **deal with** ['di:l wɪð]	sich kümmern um	68
to **decide** [dɪ'saɪd]	(sich) entscheiden	62, 68
decision [dɪ'sɪʒn]	Entscheidung	62
department store [dɪ'pɑ:tmənt ,stɔ:]	Kaufhaus	38, 47
to **depend** [dɪ'pend]	darauf ankommen	58
details ['di:teɪlz]	(Adress-)Daten, Angaben	10
different ['dɪfrnt]	anders; andere/r/s	80
directions [daɪ'rekʃnz]	Wegbeschreibung	47
to **discuss** [dɪ'skʌs]	diskutieren	70
to **do the washing** [,du: ðə 'wɒʃɪŋ]	die Wäsche machen	30
downstairs [,daʊn'steəz]	unten (im Haus)	31
to **draw** [drɔ:]	zeichnen	71
driving lessons ['draɪvɪŋ ,lesnz]	Fahrstunden	42
driving licence ['draɪvɪŋ ,laɪsns]	Führerschein	44
drummer ['drʌmə]	Schlagzeuger/in	14
to **dry** [draɪ]	trocknen	8

E

earphones ['ɪəfəʊnz]	Ohrhörer	8
electrician [,ɪlek'trɪʃn]	Elektriker/in	80
employee [ɪm'plɔɪi:]	Angestellte/r	46
engine ['endʒɪn]	Motor; Maschine	68
enough [ɪ'nʌf]	genug	27, 80
to **enter** ['entə]	eingeben	11
enthusiastic [ɪn,θju:zɪ'æstɪk]	engagiert	59
Europe ['jʊərəp]	Europa	78
even ['i:vn]	sogar	68
excited [ɪk'saɪtɪd]	aufgeregt	78
to **expect** [ɪk'spekt]	erwarten	50
experience [ɪk'spɪərɪəns]	Erfahrung	59

F

fabric ['fæbrɪk]	Stoff	38
favourite ['feɪvrɪt]	Lieblings-	6
feeling ['fi:lɪŋ]	Gefühl	20
female ['fi:meɪl]	weiblich	23
field [fi:ld]	Feld	11
firm [fɜ:m]	Firma	22
first name [,fɜ:st‿'neɪm]	Vorname	82
flat [flæt]	Wohnung	31
flat hunting ['flæt ,hʌntɪŋ]	Wohnungssuche	32
we flew [wi 'flu:]	wir flogen (Grundform: to fly)	42
flight [flaɪt]	Flug	43
floor [flɔ:]	Etage, Stockwerk	31
florist ['flɒrɪst]	Florist/in	66
fluently [flu:əntli]	fließend	59
to **follow** ['fɒləʊ]	folgen, befolgen	46
football match ['fʊtbɔ:l ,mætʃ]	Fußballspiel	18
form [fɔ:m]	Form; Formular	14
to **form** [fɔ:m]	bilden	82
Formula One [,fɔ:mjələ 'wʌn]	Formel Eins	66
French [frentʃ]	Französisch	26
friendship ['frendʃɪp]	Freundschaft	23
full-time [,fʊl'taɪm]	Ganztags-	70
furnished ['fɜ:nɪʃt]	möbliert	32
furniture ['fɜ:nɪtʃə]	Möbel	32

G

gardener ['gɑ:dnə]	Gärtner/in	66
gender ['dʒendə]	Geschlecht	23
to **get off** [,get‿'ɒf]	aussteigen	46
to **get (to ...)** ['get‿tə]	(nach ...) kommen, gelangen	46
girlfriend ['gɜ:lfrend]	(feste) Freundin	19
to **give somebody a call** [,gɪv ,sʌmbədɪ‿ə 'kɔ:l]	jemanden anrufen	78
glad [glæd]	froh	68
gladly ['glædli]	gern	56
Go ahead. [,gəʊ‿ə'hed]	Mach nur./Machen Sie nur.	22
Go on. [gəʊ‿'ɒn]	Nur zu. Mach(en Sie) schon.	8
to **grab** [græb]	packen, grapschen	51
greeting ['gri:tɪŋ]	Begrüßung	87
guest [gest]	Gast	63, 79

H

hairdresser ['heəˌdresə]	Friseur/in	8
to **hang out** [hæŋ 'aʊt]	„abhängen“	6
hard [hɑ:d]	hart	80
headphones ['hedfəʊnz]	Kopfhörer	8
Here you are. [ˌhɪə jʊ‿'ɑ:]	Hier, bitte.	34
hiking trip ['haɪkɪŋ ˌtrɪp]	Wandertour	43
to **hit** [hɪt]	stoßen, treffen	83
hole [həʊl]	Loch	83
how to write ... [ˌhaʊ tə 'raɪt]	wie man ... schreibt	56

I

I would [aɪ 'wʊd]	ich würde	56
I'd like ... [aɪd‿'laɪk]	Ich hätte gern ...	35
idiotic [ˌɪdɪ'ɒtɪk]	idiotisch	20
if I were you, I'd ... [ɪf‿aɪ wə 'ju:]	an Ihrer Stelle würde ich ...	58
immediately [ɪ'mi:diətli]	sofort	62
immigrant ['ɪmɪgrnt]	Immigrant/in, Einwanderer/in	80
in front of [ɪn 'frʌnt‿əv]	vor	47
in time [ɪn 'taɪm]	rechtzeitig, pünktlich	46
in touch [ɪn 'tʌtʃ]	in Verbindung	18
including [ɪn'klu:dɪŋ]	einschließlich	20
Indian ['ɪndiən]	indisch	80
instead of [ɪn'sted‿əv]	statt	44
interested in ['ɪntrəstɪd ɪn]	interessiert an	23
to **iron** [aɪən]	bügeln	30
Italy ['ɪtəli]	Italien	79

J

job interview ['dʒɒb ˌɪntəvju:]	Vorstellungsgespräch	20
to **join** [dʒɔɪn]	(sich) anschließen	82
joke [dʒəʊk]	Witz	10
junior reporter [ˌdʒu:nɪə rɪ'pɔ:tə]	Nachwuchsreporter/in	18
just [dʒʌst]	gerade, soeben	30

K

to **keep in touch** [ˌki:p‿ɪn 'tʌtʃ]	in Kontakt bleiben	78
to **keep your mouth shut** [ˌki:p jə 'maʊθ ˌʃʌt]	den Mund halten	70

L

language ['læŋgwɪdʒ]	Sprache	54
least serious [ˌli:st 'sɪəriəs]	am wenigsten ernst gemeint	70
leather ['leðə]	Leder	58
to **leave** [li:v]	verlassen	62
look ['lʊk]	Aussehen	58
to **look after** [ˌlʊk‿'ɑ:ftə]	betreuen	56
to **look forward to hearing from ...** [lʊk ˌfɔ:wəd‿tə 'hɪərɪŋ frəm]	sich darauf freuen, von ... zu hören	56
looking for ['lʊkɪŋ fɔ:]	auf der Suche nach	23
lorry ['lɒri]	LKW	42
lunch break ['lʌntʃ ˌbreɪk]	Mittagspause	22

M

machine operator [mə'ʃi:n ˌɒpəreɪtə]	Maschinenführer/in	22
to **make contact** [ˌmeɪk‿'kɒntækt]	Kontakt herstellen, ansprechen	38
to **make friends** [meɪk 'frendz]	Freundschaften schließen	20
male [meɪl]	männlich	23
management assistant [ˌmænɪdʒmənt ə'sɪstənt]	Bürokauffrau/-mann	22
marmalade ['mɑ:məleɪd]	Marmelade aus Zitrusfrüchten	80
to **marry** ['mæri]	heiraten	68
meal [mi:l]	Essen, Mahlzeit	30
meaningful ['mi:nɪŋfəl]	aussagekräftig	10
member ['membə]	Mitglied	14
membership ['məmbəʃɪp]	Mitgliedschaft	20
message ['mesɪdʒ]	Nachricht, Botschaft	14
to **mind** [maɪnd]	etwas dagegen haben	22
to **miss** [mɪs]	vermissen	68
motorbike ['məʊtəbaɪk]	Motorrad	26
to **move out** [mu:v 'aʊt]	ausziehen	32
mustn't ['mʌsnt]	nicht dürfen	46

N

nail polish ['neɪl ˌpɒlɪʃ]	Nagellack	34
native speaker [ˌneɪtɪv 'spi:kə]	Muttersprachler/in	59
necessary ['nesəsri]	nötig	46
neighbour ['neɪbə]	Nachbar/in	19
next to ['nekst‿tə]	neben	27, 47
normally ['nɔ:məlɪ]	normalerweise	50
not ... any more [ˌnɒt ... ˌeni'mɔ:]	nicht mehr	54
not yet [nɒt 'jet]	noch nicht	22
note [nəʊt]	Notiz	63
to **notice** ['nəʊtɪs]	bemerken	80

Word list

O

on the left [ˌɒn ðə 'left]	links	27
on the move [ˌɒn ðə 'mu:v]	in Bewegung	42
opportunity [ˌɒpə'tju:nəti]	Möglichkeit, Gelegenheit	54
opposite ['ɒpəzɪt]	gegenüber (von)	47
oven ['ʌvn]	Backofen	20
over ['əʊvə]	vorbei	68, 78
over here / over there [ˌəʊvə 'hɪə / ˌəʊvə 'ðeə]	hier / dort	34
own [əʊn]	eigene/r/s	26, 54

P

paint [peɪnt]	Farbe	34
to **paint** [peɪnt]	malen, anstreichen	34
paintbrush ['peɪntbrʌʃ]	Farbpinsel	34
parcel ['pɑ:sl]	Paket	71
to **pass** [pɑ:s]	bestehen	8
patient ['peɪʃnt]	geduldig	63, 71
pay [peɪ]	Bezahlung, Gehalt	22
perhaps [pə'hæps]	vielleicht	22
personal assistant [ˌpɜ:sənl‿ə'sɪstənt]	persönliche/r Assistent/in	56
phone box ['fəʊnbɒks]	Telefonzelle	44
phrase [freɪz]	Redewendung, Ausdruck	10
to **pick somebody up** [ˌpɪk 'ʌp]	jemanden abholen	43
pint [paɪnt]	„Halbe“ (0,568 Liter)	82
a place of my own [ə ˌpleɪs‿əv maɪ‿'əʊn]	meine eigene Bleibe	30
plant [plɑ:nt]	Pflanze	35
to **plant** [plɑ:nt]	(ein)pflanzen	66
pleased [pli:zd]	zufrieden	68
plumber ['plʌmə]	Installateur/in, Anlagen-mechaniker/in für Sanitär-, Heizungs- und Klimatechnik	80
Poland ['pəʊlənd]	Polen	80
political views [pəˌlɪtɪkl 'vju:z]	politische Einstellung	23
position [pə'zɪʃn]	(Arbeits-)Stelle	56
possible ['pɒsəbl]	möglich	82
to **post something** [pəʊst]	etwas ins Internet stellen	18
to **practise** ['præktɪs]	üben	63
to **present** [prɪ'zent]	vorstellen, präsentieren	10
probation [prə'beɪʃn]	Probezeit	68
to **produce** [prə'dju:s]	herstellen, produzieren	71
production [prə'dʌkʃn]	Produktion	22
profile ['prəʊfaɪl]	Profil, Selbstdarstellung	18
to **promise** ['prɒmɪs]	versprechen	56
to **provide** [prə'vaɪd]	anbieten	59
pub [pʌb]	Kneipe	27, 47
public transport [ˌpʌblɪk 'trænspɔ:t]	öffentlicher Nahverkehr	46

Q

qualification [ˌkwɒlɪfɪ'keɪʃn]	Qualifikation; Voraussetzung	56
queue [kju:]	(Warte-)Schlange	82
queuing ['kju:ɪŋ]	Schlange stehen	82
quite [kwaɪt]	ziemlich	44

R

racing ['reɪsɪŋ]	(Motor-)Rennen	66
rat [ræt]	Ratte	32
real [rɪəl]	echt, wirklich	20
reasons of hygiene [ˌri:znz‿əv 'haɪdʒi:n]	hygienische Gründe	20
to **receive** [rɪ'si:v]	erhalten	8
to **recommend** [ˌrekə'mend]	empfehlen	51, 58
to **register (with)** ['redʒɪstə]	sich anmelden (bei)	11
relationship [rɪ'leɪʃnʃɪp]	Beziehung	23
to **rent** [rent]	mieten	42
required [rɪ'kwaɪəd]	erforderlich	11
requirement [rɪ'kwaɪəmənt]	Anforderung	56
right [raɪt]	Recht	70
right now [ˌraɪt‿'naʊ]	im Augenblick	30
right through [ˌraɪt‿'θru:]	direkt durch	46
ringtone ['rɪŋtəʊn]	Klingelton	8
rule [ru:l]	Regel, Vorschrift	8

S

salad ['sæləd]	Salat	31
salesperson ['seɪlzˌpɜ:sn]	Verkaufsangestellte/r	59
salon ['sælɒn]	Friseursalon	54
satnav ['sætnæv]	Satellitennavigations-system, „Navi“	44
to **save** [seɪv]	sparen	66
Say hi to … from me. [ˌseɪ 'haɪ tə … frəm‿mi]	Grüße … von mir.	78
to **select** [sɪ'lekt]	auswählen	11
to **serve** [sɜ:v]	bedienen; servieren	66
to **shake** [ʃeɪk]	zittern	32
to **shake hands** [ˌʃeɪk 'hændz]	Hände schütteln, sich die Hand geben	82
shape [ʃeɪp]	Form	80
to **share** [ʃeə]	teilen	20
shelf, shelves [ʃelf, ʃelvz]	Regal, Regale	32
(shop) assistant ['ʃɒp‿əˌsɪstənt]	Verkäufer/in	34
shower [ʃaʊə]	Dusche	80
singer ['sɪŋə]	Sänger/in	6
single ['sɪŋgl]	einzig	68
size [saɪz]	Größe	34
skill [skɪl]	Fähigkeit, Fertigkeit	59
skirt [skɜ:t]	Rock	58

small talk ['smɔ:l ˌtɔ:k]	Geplauder	82
smart [smɑ:t]	schick	58
smell [smel]	Geruch	32
social network [ˌsəʊʃl 'netwɜ:k]	soziales Netzwerk	18
solar panel [ˌsəʊlə 'pænl]	Sonnenkollektor	80
to **sort** [sɔ:t]	sortieren	71
to **sound** [saʊnd]	sich anhören	54
Spain [speɪn]	Spanien	42
special ['speʃl]	besondere/r/s	58
to **spend** [spend]	ausgeben	58
status ['steɪtəs]	Status	23
still [stɪl]	immer noch	30
straight ahead [ˌstreɪt‿ə'hed]	geradeaus	47
subject ['sʌbdʒɪkt]	Betreff	10
such a … ['sʌtʃ‿ə]	so ein/e/en …	68
suit [su:t]	Anzug; Kostüm	55
to **suit somebody** [su:t]	jemandem gut stehen	58
surprised [sə'praɪzd]	überrascht	50, 58
Sweden ['swi:dn]	Schweden	78
Swedish ['swi:dɪʃ]	Schwedisch	78

T

to **take a photo** [ˌteɪk ə 'fəʊtəʊ]	ein Foto machen	27
to **take off** [ˌteɪk‿'ɒf]	ausziehen	83
technical ['teknɪkl]	technisch	71
technology [tek'nɒlədʒɪ]	Technologie	44
test drive ['test‿draɪv]	Probefahrt	68
text [tekst]	SMS	8
to **text** [tekst]	eine SMS-Nachricht verschicken, „simsen"	8
that's why [ˌðæts 'waɪ]	deshalb	68
they would like [ˌðeɪ wʊd 'laɪk]	sie hätten gern	8
thin [θɪn]	dünn	70
thought [θɔ:t]	Gedanke	20
three weeks ago [θri: 'wi:ks‿əgəʊ]	vor drei Wochen	46
through [θru:]	durch	78
to **tick** [tɪk]	ankreuzen, abhaken	11
tie [taɪ]	Krawatte	58
title ['taɪtl]	Anrede	11
Too bad. [ˌtu: 'bæd]	Schade.	32
to **touch** [tʌtʃ]	berühren	66
tour guide ['tʊə‿gaɪd]	Reiseleiter/in	59
traffic ['træfɪk]	Verkehr	82
training ['treɪnɪŋ]	Schulung, Einarbeitung	59
travel agency ['trævl‿eɪdʒənsi]	Reisebüro	59
truck [trʌk]	LKW	42
Turkey ['tɜ:ki]	die Türkei	50
to **turn left/right** [tɜ:n 'left/'raɪt]	links/rechts abbiegen	46
to **turn on** [tɜ:n 'ɒn]	einschalten, anmachen	6

U

unfortunately [ʌn'fɔ:tʃənətlɪ]	leider	20
to **unpack** [ʌn'pæk]	auspacken	38
unusual [ʌn'ju:ʒʊəl]	ungewöhnlich	35
upstairs [ʌp'steəz]	oben (im Haus)	31
used [ju:zd]	gebraucht	44

V

van [væn]	(Klein-)Transporter	42

W

wall [wɔ:l]	(Pinn-)Wand	23
wall [wɔ:l]	Wand, Mauer	67
to **warn** [wɔ:n]	warnen	82
to **wash the dishes** [ˌwɒʃ ðə 'dɪʃɪz]	abwaschen, spülen	30
to **waste** [weɪst]	verschwenden	62
a waste of time [ə ˌweɪst‿əv 'taɪm]	Zeitverschwendung	70
welcome ['welkəm]	willkommen	71
Well done! [ˌwel'dʌn]	Gut gemacht!	8
What would you like? [ˌwɒt wʊd jʊ 'laɪk]	Was wünschen Sie?	35
while [waɪl]	Weile	78
widow ['wɪdəʊ]	Witwe	32
wife [waɪf]	Ehefrau	68
to **wonder** ['wʌndə]	sich fragen	10
wood [wʊd]	Holz	34
the worst flat [ðə ˌwɜ:st 'flæt]	die schlimmste Wohnung	32
to **wrap** [ræp]	einwickeln	38
wreck [rek]	Wrack	43

Y

you should [ju 'ʃʊd]	du solltest	46
Yours sincerely [ˌjɔ:z‿sɪn'sɪəlɪ]	Mit freundlichen Grüßen	10

A

a/an	ein/e
a little	ein wenig
a lot	viel/e
a.m.	vormittags (nach Uhrzeiten)
about	über, um, ungefähr
across	(quer) über (hinüber)
address	Adresse
after	nach, nachdem
afternoon	Nachmittag
again	wieder
air	Luft
airport	Flughafen
all	alle/s
all right	in Ordnung
alone	allein
always	immer
and	und
angry	böse, wütend
animal	Tier
answer	Antwort
to **answer**	antworten
any	irgendein/e/er
apple	Apfel
arm	Arm
around	um (herum), ungefähr
to **arrive**	ankommen
to **ask (questions)**	fragen
at	an, auf, in, bei, zu
aunt	Tante
away	weg

B

back	zurück
bad	schlecht, böse
bag	Tasche
ball	Ball
banana	Banane
bank	Bank (Geldinstitut)
bathroom	Badezimmer
to **be, (was, been)**	sein
beautiful	schön
because	weil
bed	Bett
bedroom	Schlafzimmer
before	vor, bevor
to **begin, (began, begun)**	anfangen, beginnen
beginning	Anfang, Beginn
behind	hinter
big	groß
bike	Fahrrad
bird	Vogel
birthday	Geburtstag
black	schwarz
blue	blau
boat	Boot
body	Körper
book	Buch
bored	gelangweilt
boring	langweilig
bottle	Flasche
box	Karton, Schachtel
boy	Junge
bread	Brot
to **break, (broke, broken)**	(zer)brechen, kaputt machen
breakfast	Frühstück
to **bring, (brought, brought)**	bringen
brother	Bruder
brown	braun
building	Gebäude
bus, busses	Bus, Busse
business	Geschäft
busy	beschäftigt
but	aber
to **buy, (bought, bought)**	kaufen
by	durch, mit

C

cake	Kuchen
call	Anruf
to **call**	(an)rufen, nennen, heißen
can	können
cannot (can't)	nicht können
cap	Kappe
car	Auto
card	Karte
careful	vorsichtig
to **carry**	tragen
cat	Katze
to **catch, (caught, caught)**	fangen
centimetre	Zentimeter
centre	Zentrum, Mitte
chair	Stuhl
to **change**	ändern, verändern
cheap	billig
to **check**	(über)prüfen, kontrollieren
cheese	Käse
chicken	Hähnchen
child, children	Kind, Kinder
chocolate	Schokolade
Christmas	Weihnachten
cigarette	Zigarette
city	Stadt

class	(Schul)Klasse
classroom	Klassenzimmer
clean	sauber
to **clean**	reinigen, putzen
clever	klug, schlau, clever
clock	Uhr
closed	geschlossen
coach	Reisebus; Trainer/in
coffee	Kaffee
cold	kalt
colour	Farbe
to **come, (came, come)**	kommen
cook	Koch, Köchin
to **cook**	kochen
correct	korrekt, richtig
to **correct**	korrigieren
to **cost, (cost, cost)**	kosten
could	könnte/n, konnte/n
country	Land
cousin	Cousin/e
cow	Kuh
to **cry**	weinen
cup	Tasse
cut	Schnitt
to **cut, (cut, cut)**	schneiden

D

dad	Papa
dance	Tanz
to **dance**	tanzen
dangerous	gefährlich
date	Datum, Zeitpunkt, Verabredung
daughter	Tochter
day	Tag
dead	tot
dear	lieb
deep	tief
desk	Schreibtisch
to **die**	sterben
difficult	schwierig, schwer
dinner	Abendessen
dirty	schmutzig
discussion	Gespräch, Diskussion
to **do, (did, done)**	machen, tun
doctor	Arzt, Ärztin
dog	Hund
door	Tür
down	(nach) unten
to **download**	herunterladen
dream	Traum
to **dream**	träumen
dress	Kleid
drink	Getränk
to **drink, (drank, drunk)**	trinken
to **drive, (drove, driven)**	fahren
driver	Fahrer/in
dry	trocken

E

ear	Ohr
early	früh
easy	leicht
to **eat, (ate, eaten)**	essen
empty	leer
to **empty**	leeren
end	Ende, Schluss
to **end**	(be)enden
England	England
English	englisch
evening	Abend
every	jede/r/s
everybody	jeder, alle
everything	alles
exact	genau
exam	Prüfung
example	Beispiel
exciting	aufregend, spannend
exercise	Übung
expensive	teuer
to **explain**	erklären
eye	Auge

F

face	Gesicht
fall	Sturz
to **fall, (fell, fallen)**	fallen
false	falsch
family	Familie
famous	berühmt
fantastic	fantastisch
fast	schnell
fat	dick, fett
father	Vater
to **feel, (felt, felt)**	fühlen
film	Film
to **find, (found, found)**	finden
fine	fein, schön, gut
finger	Finger
to **finish**	beenden, aufhören
first	erste/r/s, zuerst
fish	Fisch
to **fish**	fischen
flower	Blume
food	Essen, Nahrung, Lebensmittel

foot, feet	Fuß, Füße
football	Fußball
for	für
to **forget, (forgot, forgotten)**	vergessen
form	Form
to **form**	formen, gestalten
free	frei, kostenlos
friend	Freund/in
friendly	freundlich
from	von, aus
fruit	Obst, Frucht
full (of)	voll (von, mit)
fun	Spaß
funny	lustig, komisch

G

game	Spiel
garage	Autowerkstatt, Garage
garden	Garten
to **get, (got, got)**	bekommen, erhalten, werden
to **get up**	aufstehen
girl	Mädchen
to **give, (gave, given)**	geben
glass	Glas
to **go, (went, gone)**	gehen, fahren
good	gut
goodbye	auf Wiedersehen
grandfather	Großvater
grandmother	Großmutter
grass	Gras
great	groß, großartig
green	grün
group	Gruppe
to **grow (grew, grown)**	wachsen

H

hair	Haar
half	halb
hand	Hand
to **happen**	passieren, geschehen
happy	glücklich
to **hate**	hassen
to **have (got), (had, had)**	haben
to **have to**	müssen
head	Kopf
to **hear, (heard, heard)**	hören
heavy	schwer
hello	hallo
help	Hilfe
to **help**	helfen
here	hier
high	hoch
hobby	Hobby
holiday	Urlaub, Ferien
home	Zuhause
at home	zu Hause
homework	Hausaufgaben
hope	Hoffnung
to **hope**	hoffen
horse	Pferd
hospital	Krankenhaus
hot	heiß, scharf
hotel	Hotel
hour	Stunde
house	Haus
how	wie
how much	wie viel
how old	wie alt
hungry	hungrig

I

ice cream	Eiskrem
idea	Idee, Vorstellung
if	wenn, falls, ob
ill	krank
important	wichtig
in	in
information	Informationen
interest	Interesse
interesting	interessant
into	in (... hinein)
to **invite (for)**	einladen (zu)

J

jacket	Jacke
jeans	Jeans
job	Arbeit, Beruf, Job
just	gerade, soeben

K

to **keep, (kept, kept)**	(be)halten, aufbewahren
to **kick**	kicken, treten
kid	Kind; Jugendliche/r
to **kill**	töten, umbringen
kilo(gramme)	Kilo(gramm)
kilometre	Kilometer
kiss	Kuss
to **kiss**	küssen
kitchen	Küche
to **know, (knew, known)**	wissen, kennen

L

last	letzte/r/s
late	spät
to **laugh**	lachen
to **learn**	lernen
left	links; übrig
lesson	Unterrichtsstunde
to **let (let, let)**	lassen
letter	Brief; Buchstabe
to **lie (down)**	(sich hin)legen, liegen
life, lives	Leben
light	hell, leicht
light	Licht, Lampe
like	wie
to **like**	mögen
line	Linie, Zeile
list	Liste
to **listen (to)**	(zu)hören
litre	Liter
little	klein, wenig
to **live**	leben, wohnen
living room	Wohnzimmer
lonely	einsam
long	lang
look	Blick
to **look**	schauen, (aus)sehen
loud	laut
love	Liebe
to **love**	lieben
lucky	glücklich
lunch	Mittagessen

M

machine	Maschine, Gerät, Automat
magazine	Zeitschrift
to **make, (made, made)**	machen, herstellen
man, men	Mann, Männer; Mensch
many	viele
map	Landkarte, Karte
to **match**	zuordnen
to **mean (meant, meant)**	meinen; bedeuten
to **meet (met, met)**	treffen; kennen lernen
metal	Metall
metre	Meter
middle	Mitte; mittlere/r/s
milk	Milch
minute	Minute
mistake	Fehler
mobile (phone)	Handy, Mobiltelefon
modern	modern
(at the) moment	(im) Moment
money	Geld
month	Monat
more	mehr
morning	Morgen
most	meiste/r/s, die meisten
mother	Mutter
mountain	Berg
mouth	Mund
much	viel
mum	Mama, Mutter
music	Musik
must	müssen

N

name	Name
to **need**	brauchen, benötigen
nervous	nervös, ängstlich
never	nie(mals)
new	neu
news	Nachricht/en, Neuigkeit
newspaper	Zeitung
next	nächste/r/s
nice	nett, schön, hübsch, gut
night	Nacht
no	kein/e; nein
nobody	niemand
not	nicht
nothing	nichts
now	jetzt
number	Zahl, Nummer

O

o'clock	Uhr (Zeitangabe)
of	von, aus, bei
of course	natürlich
off	aus, weg, von
to **offer**	anbieten
offer	Angebot
office	Büro
often	oft, häufig
old	alt
on	auf; an-, eingeschaltet
one	ein/e/er
only	nur, erst
open	offen, geöffnet
to **open**	öffnen
opposite	Gegenteil
or	oder
order	Bestellung, Befehl; Reihenfolge
to **order**	bestellen, befehlen
to **organize**	ordnen; organisieren
other	andere/r/s
out	aus
over	mehr als, über

P

p.m.	nachmittags (nach Uhrzeiten)
to **pack**	packen, einpacken
page	Seite
pair	Paar
paper	Papier
parents	Eltern
park	Park
to **park**	parken
parking	Parken
partner	Partner/in
party	Party
passenger	Passagier/in, Fahrgast
pay	Lohn, Bezahlung
to **pay, (paid, paid)**	(be)zahlen
pen	Stift, Füller
pencil	Bleistift
people	Leute, Volk
person	Person
phone	Telefon
to **phone**	anrufen, telefonieren
photo(graph)	Foto
to **pick**	aussuchen, wählen
picture	Bild
pig	Schwein
pink	rosa, pink
place	Platz, Ort, Stelle
plan	Plan
to **plan**	planen
plane	Flugzeug
plastic	(aus) Plastik
play	Theaterstück
to **play**	spielen
player	Spieler/in
please	bitte
pocket	Tasche
police	Polizei
police officer	Polizist/in
policeman	Polizist
polite	höflich
poor	arm
popular	beliebt
post office	Post
postcard	Postkarte
potato	Kartoffel
power	Macht; Stärke
present	Geschenk
press	Presse
to **press**	drücken, pressen
price	Preis
problem	Problem
programme	Programm
to **pronounce**	aussprechen
to **pull**	ziehen
pupil	Schüler/in
to **push**	schieben, stoßen
to **put, (put, put)**	setzen, stellen, legen
to **put on**	anziehen, auftragen, aufsetzen

Q

question	Frage
quick	schnell
quiet	ruhig

R

radio	Radio
rain	Regen
to **rain**	regnen
rainy	regnerisch
to **read, (read, read)**	lesen
ready	fertig, bereit
really	wirklich, eigentlich
red	rot
to **relax**	(sich) entspannen
to **remember**	sich erinnern an, daran denken
to **repair**	reparieren
report	Bericht
to **report**	berichten
rest	Rest, Ruhe
restaurant	Restaurant
rich	reich
to **ride, (rode, ridden)**	reiten, fahren
to **ride a bike**	Rad fahren
right	richtig, rechts
ring	Ring, Anruf
to **ring, (rang, rung)**	klingeln, anrufen
river	Fluss
road	Straße
room	Zimmer, Raum, Platz
round	rund
to **run, (ran, run)**	laufen, rennen

S

sad	traurig
safe	sicher
same	der-/die-/dasselbe, gleiche/r/s
sand	Sand
to **say, (said, said)**	sagen
school	Schule
sea	Meer
second	Sekunde
second	zweite/r/s
to **see, (saw, seen)**	sehen, verstehen
to **sell, (sold, sold)**	verkaufen
to **send, (sent, sent)**	schicken, senden
sentence	Satz
sheep	Schaf, Schafe

ship	Schiff
shirt	Hemd
shoe	Schuh
shop	Geschäft, Laden
shop assistant	Verkäufer/in
shopping	Einkaufen
short	kurz
to **shout**	laut rufen, schreien
show	Ausstellung, Vorstellung, Show
to **show, (showed, shown)**	zeigen
side	Seite
to **sing, (sang, sung)**	singen
single	einzel/n
sister	Schwester
to **sit, (sat, sat)**	sitzen
sleep	Schlaf
to **sleep, (slept, slept)**	schlafen
slow	langsam
small	klein
to **smile**	lächeln
smoke	Rauch
to **smoke**	rauchen
so	so
sock	Socke
soft	weich
some	einige, etwas
somebody	jemand
something	etwas
sometimes	manchmal
son	Sohn
song	Lied
soon	bald
(I'm) sorry	tut mir leid, Entschuldigung
soup	Suppe
to **speak, (spoke, spoken)**	sprechen
sport	Sport
to **stand, (stood, stood)**	stehen
start	Anfang
to **start**	anfangen, beginnen
station	Bahnhof
to **stay**	bleiben; übernachten
stop	Halt
to **stop**	beenden, anhalten, aufhören
story	Geschichte
street	Straße
strong	stark
stupid	dumm
subject	(Schul-)Fach
suddenly	plötzlich
summary	Zusammenfassung
summer	Sommer
sun	Sonne
supermarket	Supermarkt
sure	sicher
surprise	Überraschung
to **swim, (swam, swum)**	schwimmen

T

table	Tisch, Tabelle
to **take, (took, taken)**	nehmen, brauchen, dauern
to **talk**	reden, sprechen
taxi	Taxi
tea	Tee
to **teach, (taught, taught)**	unterrichten
teacher	Lehrer/in
to **tell, (told, told)**	erzählen, sagen
terrible	schrecklich, furchtbar
test	Test, Klassenarbeit
text	Text
than	als
to **thank**	(sich) bedanken
that (one)	der/die/das da
that	dass
the	der/die/das
theatre	Theater
then	dann
there	dort, da
there are/is	es gibt, es sind/ist
these	diese
thing	Ding, Sache
to **think, (thought, thought)**	denken, glauben, meinen
this	diese/r/s
those	jene
ticket	Fahr-, Eintrittskarte
time	Zeit
tip	Tipp
tired	müde
to	zu, nach; an; bis
today	heute
together	zusammen
toilet	Toilette, WC
tomato	Tomate
tomorrow	morgen
too	auch; zu
top	Spitze
tourist	Tourist/in
town	Stadt
toy	Spielzeug
train	Zug

to **train**	trainieren
to **translate**	übersetzen
to **travel**	reisen, fahren
tree	Baum
trip	Reise
trouble	Ärger
true	wahr, richtig, echt
to **try**	versuchen, (aus)probieren
TV	Fernsehen, Fernseher, Fernsehapparat

U

uncle	Onkel
under	unter
to **understand, (understood, understood)**	verstehen
until	bis
to **use**	benutzen, verwenden
usually	meistens, gewöhnlich

V

very	sehr
visit	Besuch
to **visit**	besuchen

W

to **wait (for)**	warten (auf)
to **wake up**	aufwachen
to **walk**	gehen, laufen, spazieren
to **want**	wollen
warm	warm
to **wash**	waschen
to **watch**	beobachten, zuschauen
water	Wasser
way	Weg
to **wear (wore, worn)**	tragen, anziehen
weather	Wetter
week	Woche
weekend	Wochenende
well	gut, gesund; also
what	was
what about ...	was ist mit ...
when	wann
when	als; wenn
where	wo(hin)
which	welche/r/s
white	weiß
who	wer, wem, wen
whole	ganz
why	warum
will ('ll)	werden
to **win, (won, won)**	gewinnen
window	Fenster
winter	Winter
with	mit
without	ohne
woman, women	Frau, Frauen
word	Wort
work	Arbeit
to **work**	arbeiten
world	Welt
to **write, (wrote, written)**	schreiben
to **write down**	aufschreiben
wrong	falsch

Y

year	Jahr
yellow	gelb
yes	ja
yesterday	gestern
young	jung

Z

zoo	Zoo

Bildquellennachweis

4 Corbis RF (Image Source), Düsseldorf; **4** iStockphoto (mattjeacock), Calgary, Alberta; **4** shutterstock (l i g h t p o e t), New York, NY; **4** shutterstock (Kiselev Andrey Valerevich), New York, NY; **5** iStockphoto (Plougmann), Calgary, Alberta; **5** iStockphoto (Angelika Schwarz), Calgary, Alberta; **5** Dreamstime LLC (Tyler Olson), Brentwood, TN; **6** Thinkstock (iStockphoto), München; **6** Corbis RF (Image Source), Düsseldorf; **6** shutterstock (Helga Esteb), New York, NY; **6** shutterstock (Ferenc Szelepcsenyi), New York, NY; **6** Dreamstime LLC (Andreas Gradin), Brentwood, TN; **7** Corbis (RCWW, Inc.), Düsseldorf; **7** Corbis RF (Ocean), Düsseldorf; **7** shutterstock (Dmitry Kalinovsky), New York, NY; **7** Thinkstock (iStockphoto), München; **8** Fotolia LLC (contrastwerkstatt), New York; **10** Thinkstock (Medioimages/Photodisc), München; **12** Thinkstock (Brand X Pictures/Jupiterimages), München; **12** Thinkstock (Photos.com/Jupiterimages), München; **13** Video(s) supplied by BBC Motion Gallery, London; **14** shutterstock (Sheftsoff), New York, NY; **15** Thinkstock (iStockphoto), München; **15** Thinkstock (Hemera), München; **16** Corbis (Andy Mills/Star Ledger), Düsseldorf; **18** iStockphoto (101dalmatians), Calgary, Alberta; **18** Fotosearch Stock Photography (Stockbyte), Waukesha, WI; **18** iStockphoto (mattjeacock), Calgary, Alberta; **19** shutterstock (Monkey Business Images), New York, NY; **19** shutterstock (Val Thoermer), New York, NY; **19** Thinkstock (Comstock/Jupiterimages), München; **20** Thinkstock (Pixland), München; **20** shutterstock (Valua Vitaly), New York, NY; **21** Fotolia LLC (contrastwerkstatt), New York; **22** Thinkstock (Jupiterimages), München; **24** iStockphoto (Chris Schmidt), Calgary, Alberta; **24** iStockphoto (william casey), Calgary, Alberta; **25** Video(s) supplied by BBC Motion Gallery, London; **27** shutterstock (Kiselev Andrey Valerevich), New York, NY; **28** iStockphoto (franckreporter), Calgary, Alberta; **30** Thinkstock (Creatas), München; **30** iStockphoto (Cameron Pashak), Calgary, Alberta; **30** Thinkstock (iStockphoto), München; **31** shutterstock (Redphotographer), New York, NY; **31** iStockphoto (Patrick Heagney), Calgary, Alberta; **31** Fotolia LLC (Christopher Howey), New York; **31** Corbis (Najlah Feanny), Düsseldorf; **32** shutterstock (Tupungato), New York, NY; **32** shutterstock (l i g h t p o e t), New York, NY; **32** iStockphoto (fotoVoyager), Calgary, Alberta; **33** Thinkstock (liquidlibrary/Dynamic Graphics), München; **34** shutterstock (Ralf Hahn), New York, NY; **35** Thinkstock (Brand X Pictures), München; **35** iStockphoto (Angelika Schwarz), Calgary, Alberta; **35** iStockphoto (RF/Renee Lee), Calgary, Alberta; **36** iStockphoto (James Pauls), Calgary, Alberta; **36** Thinkstock (Brand X Pictures), München; **37** Video(s) supplied by BBC Motion Gallery, London; **38** shutterstock (mangostock), New York, NY; **39** iStockphoto (JOSE JUAN GARCIA), Calgary, Alberta; **40** shutterstock (Iwona Grodzka), New York, NY; **42** shutterstock (Kiselev Andrey Valerevich), New York, NY; **42** shutterstock (Chris Driscoll), New York, NY; **42** shutterstock (Lisa F. Young), New York, NY; **43** shutterstock (bullet74), New York, NY; **43** shutterstock (riekephotos), New York, NY; **43** iStockphoto (Tom Fullum), Calgary, Alberta; **43** shutterstock (omers), New York, NY; **44** shutterstock (mangostock), New York, NY; **44** shutterstock (Four Oaks), New York, NY; **45** Thinkstock (iStockphoto), München; **46** shutterstock (Kenneth William Caleno), New York, NY; **48** shutterstock (Anton Gvozdikov), New York, NY; **48** Thinkstock (Stockbyte/George Doyle), München; **49** Video(s) supplied by BBC Motion Gallery, London; **51** iStockphoto (A-Digit), Calgary, Alberta; **52** laif (Sylvain GRANDADAM/HOA-QUI), Köln; **54** iStockphoto (Angelika Schwarz), Calgary, Alberta; **56** iStockphoto (Frank van den Bergh), Calgary, Alberta; **56** Thinkstock (iStockphoto), München; **57** iStockphoto (Alija), Calgary, Alberta; **58** shutterstock (Peter Bernik), New York, NY; **60** shutterstock (Simone van den Berg), New York, NY; **60** iStockphoto (Craig Swatton), Calgary, Alberta; **61** Video(s) supplied by BBC Motion Gallery, London; **62** Thinkstock (Stockbyte), München; **63** Thinkstock (Photodisc), München; **64** Thinkstock (iStockphoto), München; **66** shutterstock (Ivanova Inga), New York, NY; **66** iStockphoto (Tyler Stalman), Calgary, Alberta; **67** iStockphoto (Kelly Cline), Calgary, Alberta; **67** shutterstock (Alexander Raths), New York, NY; **67** iStockphoto (Eliza Snow), Calgary, Alberta; **67** Dreamstime LLC (Tyler Olson), Brentwood, TN; **67** shutterstock (Dmitry Kalinovsky), New York, NY; **67** shutterstock (lev dolgachov), New York, NY; **68** iStockphoto (Sean Locke), Calgary, Alberta; **68** shutterstock (michaeljung), New York, NY; **70** iStockphoto (Martina Barbist), Calgary, Alberta; **70** Thinkstock (Photodisc/Jack Hollingsworth), München; **70** iStockphoto (Nicholas Monu), Calgary, Alberta; **70** shutterstock (Anna Lurye), New York, NY; **70** Thinkstock (iStockphoto), München; **71** shutterstock (Rainer Plendl), New York, NY; **72** shutterstock (Lisa A), New York, NY; **72** iStockphoto (David H. Lewis), Calgary, Alberta; **73** Video(s) supplied by BBC Motion Gallery, London; **74** Thinkstock (Photos.com/Jupiterimages), München; **75** shutterstock (Santje09), New York, NY; **75** shutterstock (Losevsky Pavel), New York, NY; **76** iStockphoto (Vladimir Piskunov), Calgary, Alberta; **78** Geoatlas, Hendaye; **78** Dream Maker Software (RF), Colorado; **78** iStockphoto (Plougmann), Calgary, Alberta; **78** iStockphoto (Sara Pinnell), Calgary, Alberta; **79** iStockphoto (mayo5), Calgary, Alberta; **79** BigStockPhoto.com (liewy), Davis, CA; **79** shutterstock (Deklofenak), New York, NY; **79** iStockphoto (Lauri Patterson), Calgary, Alberta; **79** iStockphoto (Ian Hamilton), Calgary, Alberta; **80** shutterstock (grublee), New York, NY; **80** shutterstock (Benis Arapovic), New York, NY; **80** shutterstock (tiggra), New York, NY; **80** Thinkstock (iStockphoto), München; **81** Thinkstock (iStockphoto), München; **81** shutterstock (Joe Gough), New York, NY; **81** shutterstock (Voyagerix), New York, NY; **81** shutterstock (linerpics), New York, NY; **81** shutterstock (Dan70), New York, NY; **82** Thinkstock (Photodisc/Digital Vision), München; **83** Corbis (Sven Hagolani), Düsseldorf; **84** Thinkstock (Hemera), München; **85** Video(s) supplied by BBC Motion Gallery, London; **86** Thinkstock (BananaStock), München; **87** Thinkstock (Photos.com/Jupiterimages), München; **88** Thinkstock (Comstock), München; **90** iStockphoto (Nicholas Sutcliffe), Calgary, Alberta; **90** iStockphoto (photovideostock), Calgary, Alberta; **90** Thinkstock (iStockphoto), München; **90** iStockphoto (RF/Dainis Derics), Calgary, Alberta; **90** shutterstock (Monkey Business Images), New York, NY; **90** Thinkstock (Jupiterimages), München; **90** iStockphoto (RF/Photomick), Calgary, Alberta; **90** shutterstock (nikola-master), New York, NY; **91** Getty Images (Lucas Schifres/Bloomberg), München; **91** Thinkstock (iStockphoto), München; **91** iStockphoto (ROBERT WEBER), Calgary, Alberta; **91** iStockphoto (Wayne d\'Eon), Calgary, Alberta; **92** iStockphoto (Louis-Paul St-Onge), Calgary, Alberta; **92** Thinkstock (SW Productions), München; **92** Thinkstock (iStockphoto), München; **93** shutterstock (R Carner), New York, NY; **93** iStockphoto (adrian beesley), Calgary, Alberta; **93** iStockphoto (Mike Clarke), Calgary, Alberta; **93** shutterstock (Neale Cousland), New York, NY; **93** shutterstock (Maksym Dragunov), New York, NY; **93** iStockphoto (npphotos), Calgary, Alberta; **93** shutterstock (Tomas Skopal), New York, NY; **94** Thinkstock (Comstock), München; **94** shutterstock (Chubykin Arkady), New York, NY; **94** Corbis (Anouk de Maar/cultura), Düsseldorf; **94** shutterstock (mikeledray), New York, NY; **94** shutterstock (LUCARELLI TEMISTOCLE), New York, NY; **95** Thinkstock (Jupiterimages), München; **95** shutterstock (Glovatskiy), New York, NY; **95** shutterstock (ostill), New York, NY; **96** Thinkstock (Hemera), München; **96** shutterstock (Istvan Csak), New York, NY; **96** Corbis (Mark Hunt/Huntstock), Düsseldorf; **96** shutterstock (Anton Brand), New York, NY; **97** Thinkstock (Hemera), München; **97** shutterstock (Davor Pukljak), New York, NY; **97** shutterstock (ULKASTUDIO), New York, NY; **103** shutterstock (Glenda M. Powers), New York, NY; **103** shutterstock (Elena Elisseeva), New York, NY; **103** shutterstock (StockLite), New York, NY; **103** shutterstock (Toranico), New York, NY; **103** shutterstock (Iakov Filimonov), New York, NY; **103** shutterstock (OLEKSANDR SHEVCHENKO), New York, NY; **105** Thinkstock (Hemera), München; **105** Thinkstock (iStockphoto), München; **105** Thinkstock (Comstock), München; **105** Thinkstock (Brand X Pictures/Jupiterimages), München; **105** shutterstock (Vibrant Image Studio), New York, NY; **105** shutterstock (Stephen Coburn), New York, NY; **105** shutterstock (TheLightEd), New York, NY; **105** shutterstock (Val Thoermer), New York, NY; **107** Thinkstock (Valueline/Design Pics/Stock Foundry), München; **107** Thinkstock (iStockphoto), München; **107** iStockphoto (Tim Denison), Calgary, Alberta; **107** iStockphoto (Brad Wieland), Calgary, Alberta; **107** iStockphoto (Teodor Todorov), Calgary, Alberta; **109** Thinkstock (Pixland), München; **109** shutterstock (Luna Vandoorne), New York, NY; **109** shutterstock (PT Images), New York, NY; **109** shutterstock (lithian), New York, NY; **109** shutterstock (shooarts), New York, NY; **111** Klett-Archiv, Stuttgart; **111** Geoatlas, Hendaye; **111** Dream Maker Software (RF), Colorado; **111** TEBITRON GMBH, Edward Eckstein, Gerlingen; **128** Klett-Archiv, Stuttgart; **142** Klett-Archiv, Stuttgart; **143** Klett-Archiv, Stuttgart; **COVER** Thinkstock (iStockphoto), München

Sollte es in einem Einzelfall nicht gelungen sein, den korrekten Rechteinhaber ausfindig zu machen, so werden berechtigte Ansprüche selbstverständlich im Rahmen der üblichen Regelungen abgegolten.

International Boundary
Internal Boundary
LONDON National Capital
Belfast Administrative Unit Capital
LONDON over 1 000 000 inhabitants
LEEDS 500 000 – 1 000 000 inhabitants
Oxford 100 000 – 500 000 inhabitants
Cambridge under 100 000 inhabitants
Urban Area
Railway
Tunnel
Car Ferry
Motorway
Road
International Airport
Coastline
River
Lake
Canal
0 50 100 150 km
ATLANTIC OCEAN
North Sea
UNITED KINGDOM
SCOTLAND
ENGLAND
WALES
NORTHERN IRELAND
IRELAND
NETHERLANDS
BELGIUM
FRANCE
Irish Sea
English Channel
Shetland Islands
Unst
Yell
Mainland
Lerwick
Foula
Fair Isle
Orkney Islands
Westray
Sanday
Mainland
Hoy
Kirkwall
Pentland Firth
Rona
Flannan Is.
Outer Hebrides
Lewis
Stornoway
North Minch
Little Minch
St. Kilda
North Uist
South Uist
Barra
Sea of the Hebrides
Inner Hebrides
Skye
Rhum
Coll
Mull
Firth of Lorn
Jura
Islay
Arran
Firth of Clyde
North Channel
Wick
Loch Shin
Moray Firth
Inverness
Loch Ness
Spey
Dee
Aberdeen
Fort William
Tay
Dundee
Firth of Tay
Firth of Forth
Loch Lomond
Edinburgh
GLASGOW
Clyde
Tweed
Kilmarnock
Stranraer
Solway Firth
Carlisle
Eden
Tyne
Newcastle upon Tyne
Sunderland
Middlesbrough
Lough Foyle
Londonderry
Larne
L. Neagh
L. Erne
Belfast
Donegal Bay
Sligo
ISLE OF MAN
Douglas
Lancaster
York
Blackpool
Bradford
LEEDS
Kingston upon Hull
Humber
Bolton
Huddersfield
Grimsby
Liverpool
Manchester
Trent
Anglesey
Holyhead
Birkenhead
Stockport
SHEFFIELD
Achill I.
Dundalk
L. Mask
L. Ree
L. Corrib
Galway
Galway Bay
Aran Is.
Shannon
Tullamore
DUBLIN
(BAILE ÁTHA CLIATH)
Lough Derg
Limerick
Kilkenny
Barrow
Suir
Tralee
Blackwater
Waterford
Rosslare Harbour
Cork
St. George's Channel
Cardigan Bay
Fishguard
Milford Haven
Stoke-on-Trent
Derby
Nottingham
The Wash
Norwich
Great Yarmouth
Ouse
Leicester
Walsall
Wolverhampton
BIRMINGHAM
Peterborough
Coventry
Northampton
Severn
Wye
Stratford-upon-Avon
Cambridge
Ipswich
Harwich
Gloucester
Luton
Oxford
Thames
LONDON
Greenwich
Southend on Sea
Rhondda
Newport
Swansea
Cardiff
Bristol
Bath
Reading
Canterbury
Dover
Bristol Channel
Lundy
Salisbury
Hastings
Strait of Dover
Calais
Southampton
Brighton
Newhaven
Portsmouth
Exeter
Bournemouth
Isle of Wight
Torbay
Weymouth
Plymouth
Penzance
Isles of Scilly
St. Peter Port
GUERNSEY
St. Helier
JERSEY
Cherbourg
Seine Bay
Le Havre
Rouen
Seine
Beauvais
Oise
Amiens
Somme
St-Quentin
Aisne
Reims
Lille
Dunkerque
Brugge (Brugges)
Ostend
Ghent
Antwerp
BRUSSELS
Texel
Alkmaar
Haarlem
The Hague
ROTTERDAM
KLETT-PERTHES

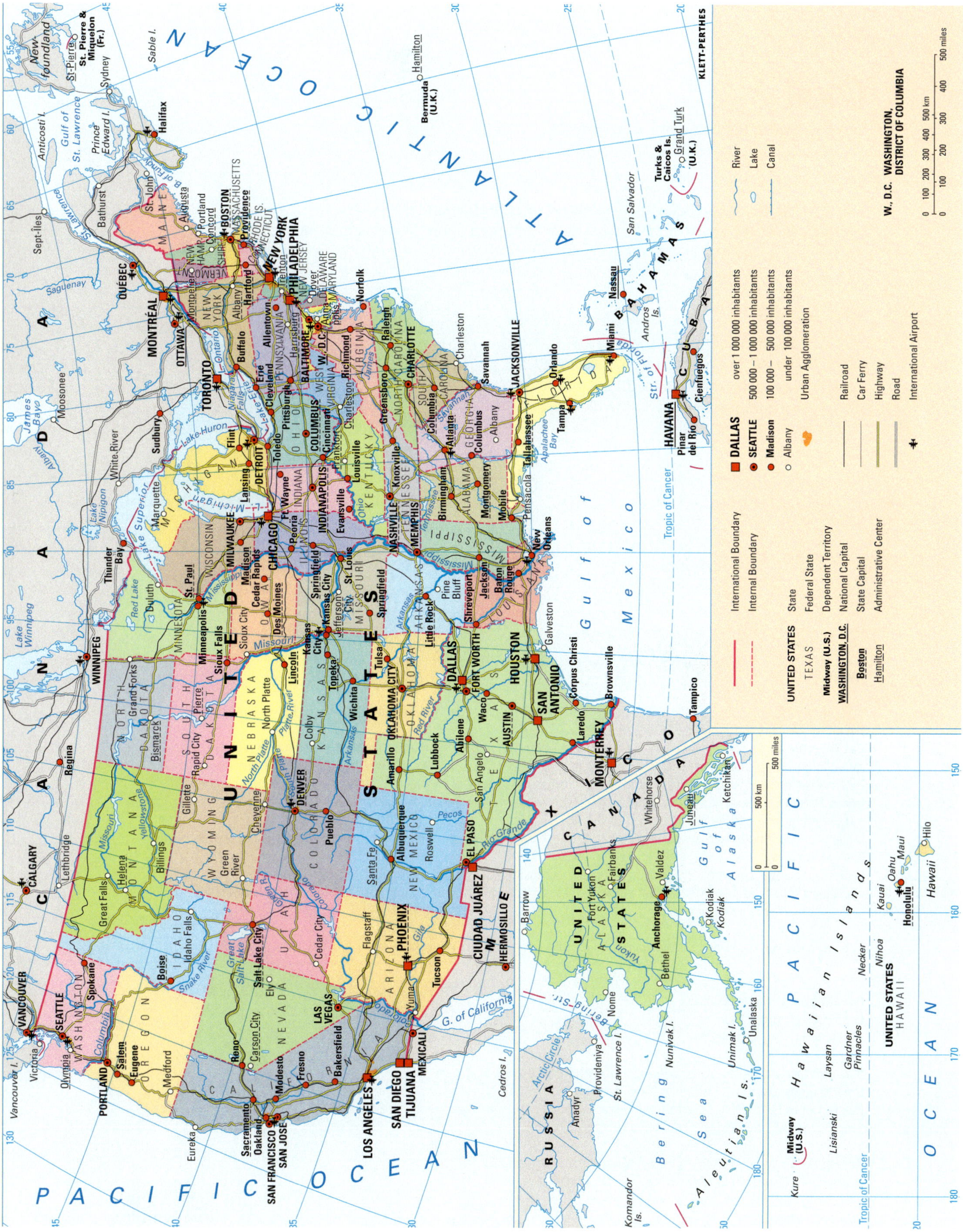
PACIFIC OCEAN
ATLANTIC OCEAN
Gulf of Mexico
CANADA
UNITED STATES
MEXICO
CUBA
BAHAMAS
RUSSIA
UNITED STATES ALASKA
UNITED STATES HAWAII
Hawaiian Islands
Bering Sea
Aleutian Is.
Gulf of Alaska
PACIFIC OCEAN
G. of California
Tropic of Cancer
WASHINGTON
OREGON
CALIFORNIA
NEVADA
IDAHO
MONTANA
WYOMING
UTAH
ARIZONA
COLORADO
NEW MEXICO
NORTH DAKOTA
SOUTH DAKOTA
NEBRASKA
KANSAS
OKLAHOMA
TEXAS
MINNESOTA
IOWA
MISSOURI
ARKANSAS
LOUISIANA
WISCONSIN
ILLINOIS
MICHIGAN
INDIANA
OHIO
KENTUCKY
TENNESSEE
MISSISSIPPI
ALABAMA
GEORGIA
FLORIDA
SOUTH CAROLINA
NORTH CAROLINA
VIRGINIA
WEST VIRGINIA
PENNSYLVANIA
NEW YORK
VERMONT
NEW HAMPSHIRE
MAINE
MASSACHUSETTS
RHODE IS.
CONNECTICUT
NEW JERSEY
DELAWARE
MARYLAND
W. D.C.
SEATTLE
PORTLAND
SAN FRANCISCO
SAN JOSE
LOS ANGELES
SAN DIEGO
TIJUANA
LAS VEGAS
PHOENIX
DENVER
EL PASO
CIUDAD JUÁREZ
DALLAS
FORT WORTH
HOUSTON
SAN ANTONIO
AUSTIN
OKLAHOMA CITY
KANSAS CITY
CHICAGO
MILWAUKEE
DETROIT
INDIANAPOLIS
COLUMBUS
MEMPHIS
NASHVILLE
CHARLOTTE
JACKSONVILLE
BALTIMORE
PHILADELPHIA
NEW YORK
BOSTON
TORONTO
MONTRÉAL
OTTAWA
QUÉBEC
WINNIPEG
CALGARY
VANCOUVER
MONTERREY
HAVANA
MEXICALI
HERMOSILLO
KLETT-PERTHES
International Boundary
Internal Boundary
UNITED STATES State
TEXAS Federal State
Midway (U.S.) Dependent Territory
WASHINGTON, D.C. National Capital
Boston State Capital
Hamilton Administrative Center
DALLAS over 1 000 000 inhabitants
SEATTLE 500 000 – 1 000 000 inhabitants
Madison 100 000 – 500 000 inhabitants
Albany under 100 000 inhabitants
Urban Agglomeration
Railroad
Car Ferry
Highway
Road
International Airport
River
Lake
Canal
W., D.C. WASHINGTON, DISTRICT OF COLUMBIA
0 100 200 300 400 500 km
0 100 200 300 400 500 miles

Cool!

Berufsvorbereitung Englisch – BEJ / VAB

von: Birgit Herrmann, Freudenstadt; Andrew K. Johnson, Cambridge
Beratung: Eva Eitel, Schwaigern; Michael Hack, Nürtingen; Tanja Weidemann, Hannover

Werkübersicht:

Cool! Lehr-/Arbeitsbuch, 978-3-12-808111-3
Keep Cool! Lehr-/Arbeitsbuch, 978-3-12-808113-7
Cool! / Keep cool! Lehrerhandbuch, 978-3-12-808112-0
Online-Ergänzungen unter www.klett.de/online

1. Auflage 1 9 8 7 6 5 | 21 20 19 18 17

Alle Drucke dieser Auflage sind unverändert und können im Unterricht nebeneinander verwendet werden.
Die letzte Zahl bezeichnet das Jahr des Druckes.

Im Lehrwerk befinden sich ausschließlich fiktive Internet-Adressen, die deshalb auch mit ww#. beginnen anstatt wie üblich mit www.
Die im Buch abgedruckten Mediencodes führen zu interaktiven Zusatzübungen und Hörverständnistexten auf www.klett.de. Die Mediencodes leiten ausschließlich zu optionalen Unterrichtsmaterialien, sie unterliegen nicht dem staatlichen Zulassungsverfahren.

Projektleitung: Matthias Rupp
Redaktion: Astrid Keller
Herstellung: Angelika Lindner

Satz und Gestaltung: B2 Büro für Gestaltung, Andreas Staiger, Stuttgart
Umschlaggestaltung: Stefanie Kaufhold, Berlin
Illustrationen: B2 Büro für Gestaltung, Andreas Staiger, Stuttgart; Jeongsook Lee, Heidelberg; Sven Palmowski, Barcelona; Chris Veit, Stuttgart

Reproduktion: Meyle + Müller Medien-Management, Pforzheim
Druck: DBM Druckhaus Berlin-Mitte GmbH, Berlin

Printed in Germany
ISBN 978-3-12-808111-3

9 783128 081113